Allied Special Forces Insignia
1939–1948

In Memory of Jim Longson 1922–1999

Allied Special Forces Insignia
1939–1948

Peter Taylor

Pen & Sword
MILITARY

First published in Great Britain in 2000 by Leo Cooper

This edition published in Great Britain in 2013 by
Pen & Sword Military
an imprint of
Pen & Sword Books Ltd
47 Church Street
Barnsley
South Yorkshire
S70 2AS

ISBN: 978-1-78159-123-9

Typeset in 11pt Ehrhardt by
Mac Style, Beverley, E. Yorkshire

Printed and bound in India by Replika Press Pvt. Ltd.

Pen & Sword Books Ltd incorporates the Imprints of Pen & Sword Aviation,
Pen & Sword Family History, Pen & Sword Maritime, Pen & Sword Military,
Pen & Sword Discovery, Wharncliffe Local History, Wharncliffe True Crime,
Wharncliffe Transport, Pen & Sword Select, Pen & Sword Military Classics,
Leo Cooper, The Praetorian Press, Remember When, Seaforth Publishing
and Frontline Publishing.

For a complete list of Pen & Sword titles please contact
PEN & SWORD BOOKS LIMITED
47 Church Street, Barnsley, South Yorkshire, S70 2AS, England
E-mail: enquiries@pen-and-sword.co.uk
Website: www.pen-and-sword.co.uk

Contents

Acknowledgements

My most grateful thanks to all the following friends and colleagues who so generously gave me their help and time over the gathering of detail and material for this book. Without that help it could never have been completed.

Robert Bragg, UK. Whose written knowledge on where and how Parachute Wings and Shoulder Titles were worn was a great help.

Andrew Bragg, UK. A great help on Special Air Service Regiment and Airborne insignia.

Michael J. Beckett, UK. His expert knowledge on Army Commandos and the loan of some of his collection was a great help.

Grenvile Bint, UK. His constant assistance in finding insignia, original documents and photographs really helped me.

John Atherton, UK. Loaned Royal Marine insignia.

Claude Ascensi, France, the French photographs.

Stuart Wright, UK. Chindit and Indian Airborne insignia.

Graham Wright, UK. Helped with purchasing original Airborne photographs.

William Gill, UK. Helped with his knowledge on Army Commandos and especially 2 Commando.

Mike Spencer, UK. Commando insignia.

Steve Mackenzie, Canada, British and Canadian Airborne.

Tom Matchett, UK. Chindit insignia.

Colonel MC Mc Henry, USA. Helped me to locate books and documents on US Special Forces.

Norman Lichfield, UK. Helped with information on Royal Artillery Units attached to Airborne Forces, and the use of insignia in his collection.

Malcolm Johnson, USA. His was the inspiration behind this book. His knowledge on all aspects of Airborne insignia and the use of his vast collection helped me a great deal.

Mike Jackson, UK. Commando and Special Air Service Regiment.

Eitan Israely, Israel. Palestinian and Jewish related insignia 1939-1945.

Len Whitaker for his help with information on the more unusual British Special Forces units.

Ian Harrison, UK. For information on insignia.

David Hiorth, Canada, for information on airborne insignia.

John Gaylor, UK.

Hugh King, UK.

Trevor Lemon, UK. For information on US insignia 1940-45.

Stuart A. Eastwood, UK. Kings Own Border Regimental Museum.

Roy L. Dupuy, USA. Help with finding US insignia.

Roy Carter, UK. Who helped me greatly with information on airborne insignia and finding airborne photographs.

Les Hughes, USA. Provided all my information on OSS and Jedburghs, also the loan of insignia.

David Buxton, UK. For the loan of photographs and information.

Diane Andrews, UK. A big thank you for her patience and help at the Airborne Forces Museum. Identifying insignia and original photographs in my collection.

The Sikorski Institute, UK. Was a great help with all aspects of Polish Airborne insignia and in helping me identify original photographs in my collection.

Jim Longson, UK. 1st Border Regiment and 1st Airlanding Brigade. Jim was a great inspiration and help in finding original documents and photographs for me.

Robert Miles, New Zealand. Helped me find photographs of the Long Range Desert Group and the Special Air Service Regiment.

Bryan Watkins, UK. For producing a highly informative Introduction which gives the background to the creation of many of the Allied Special Forces.

Cheryl Jackson, UK, whose patience in typing and double checking information for me, and giving up a lot of her free time to trail round Museums and Libraries was a great help.

Christine Taylor, UK. Who helped me make sense of some of the chapters and thoroughly checked all my grammar.

This book has taken approximately seventeen years of my life to compile and even during the final stages new information came to light. I am sure that there will be areas where further material will be forthcoming and I would encourage readers to alert me to this so that it can be included in future editions.

June 2000

Peter Taylor

Introduction

'Engage the enemy more closely'
Admiral Lord Nelson at Trafalgar

In this catalogue of Special Forces insignia, Peter Taylor has given the reader some background information on the origins and roles of the Forces he lists. This Introduction is intended to augment some of that background and to reflect something of the nature and spirit of Special Forces as a whole. The canvas to be covered was extensive and the heroic contribution made to final victory by Special Forces already fills many volumes. Here I have only sought to show a little of the way in which Special Forces were born and developed and to give the reader some feel for their character and quality. Of necessity, it has only been possible to touch on the major elements and to concentrate mainly upon the earlier years of the story. Many small forces shown in the main text have no mention, simply because of a lack of space to do them justice.

What, in fact, were Special Forces? In his excellent *British Special Forces*, William Seymour, now a distinguished military historian and a former officer of the Scots Guards, who fought as a Commando in the Middle East and Burma, has given us this definition, suggesting that the term should, strictly, be applied to:

Forces specially trained and equipped to fulfil a particular purpose for which regular formations may not be suitable or available.

He cites the Long Range Desert Group (see page 71) as a perfect example. He goes on to make this important point:

The criteria must be that such a force should not be large, should be kept well under control, should be used only for the special purpose for which it was raised and should be well disciplined.

For many reasons, that wise reservation was not always observed during the Second World War, particularly with regard to size and use, probably because there is always a tendency on the part of both commanders and staffs to put their money on any element under command which has proved to be particularly effective in battle. Even since that war, whenever the whistle has blown, it has been a safe bet that the Parachute Regiment and the Royal Marine Commandos will be first down on any Order of Battle even though the task is essentially one for conventional infantry.

Winston Churchill's stirring and unforgettable speeches to the British public in June and July, 1940, did much to salvage national morale after Dunkirk and to reassure our Allies and the Free World of our determination to fight on, despite the overwhelming odds we faced. Nevertheless, golden though those words may have been, both the Prime Minister himself and the Chiefs of Staff realized how important it had become that practical proof of that determination should be given through offensive action. Hence Churchill's directive to '*set Europe alight*'.

With the Army in tatters and shorn of much of its heavy weapons and equipment, let alone its supplies of ammunition, the $64,000 question was how that directive could be implemented with the resources available. It was not public morale alone that was at stake but a deep need to enable the Army to regain its self-respect, keenly aware as its officers and soldiers were that they had suffered a humiliating defeat at the hands of a very tough enemy.

Both the Royal Navy and the Royal Air Force were already engaged in operations of one sort or another and not long before Dunkirk, the RN had reduced the Germans' existing destroyer forces by fifty per cent in fierce fighting off Norway. The RAF, soon to inflict a stunning defeat upon Goering's *Luftwaffe* in the Battle of Britain, was determined to carry the air war into the heart of Germany. Although the Army was preparing to do battle in the Western Desert with the Italians, at home there was only one course open to them – raiding against enemy held coastlines and some form of clandestine operations within the boundaries of Occupied Europe. If raiding was indeed to be the name of the game, something radical had to be developed.

The immediate problem was the threat of invasion, for which Hitler had evolved his Operation *See Loewe* and was busily gathering shipping for that purpose. However, the Navy's control of the Channel and the coastal waters of the North Sea and the RAF's victory in the Battle of Britain, together with the realization by the Germans that the invasion barges which the RAF were constantly strafing were quite inadequate for a serious seaborne assault, gradually persuaded Hitler that *See Loewe* was no longer a starter, and the threat was seriously diminished. Now, at last, the Army could think seriously of mounting limited offensive operations – given the men and the right resources. Both the other Services would provide any support required.

Early in 1940, some months before the end of the 'phoney war' in France, the efforts of Major J.EC. Holland, a Sapper working on Intelligence research, were rewarded by the authorization of the formation of ten Independent Companies whose task was to be the raiding of the Germans' Lines of Communication. The men were drawn principally from the Territorial Divisions and were all volunteers. The invasion of Norway by the Germans in April and the despatch of a small Allied force to the Narvik area saw five of these companies, commanded by Lieutenant

Colonel Colin Gubbins, being dispatched with that force. When they got there, the shortage of infantry was such that the Companies were pitchforked into battle as infantrymen and were unable to exercise their special skills. Despite this unsatisfactory misuse of Britain's first Special Forces, their very creation had set a vital precedent and, within weeks, Colonel Dudley Clarke, the Military Assistant to General Sir John Dill, the Chief of the Imperial General Staff, had produced a plan, which had long been hatching in his mind, to establish a number of raiding units, which he christened Commandos after the Boer raiding forces in the South African War. He put his paper to his Chief and received almost immediate permission to go ahead. After the Norwegian fiasco, the Independent Companies were earmarked for disbandment, thereby giving Dudley Clarke an excellent pool of high class, trained men upon which to found his first Commandos.

One severe restraint was imposed upon Clarke – nothing could be issued to the Commandos which might inhibit the redevelopment of the Home Army or was needed for General Wavell's Middle East Command. Despite this handicap, Clarke's units began to train with what Seymour calls '*an assortment of shared weapons*' and to plan two small raids – one against a German airfield near Le Touquet and the other against the island of Guernsey. Seymour comments that '*Both these raids were poor harbingers of what was to come but they taught valuable lessons and the publicity they achieved was good for recruiting.*'

In August, 1940, Admiral of the Fleet Sir Roger Keyes, the hero of the Dover Patrol in the First World War and a great fighter, who had returned to the Admiralty 'to do his bit' in 1939 and now held the post of Director of Combined Operations, gripped the Commando training problem by concentrating all the newly formed units at the Combined Training Centre at Inveraray. The men accepted for training were all trained infantry soldiers, volunteers and, with some exceptions, of high quality. The twelve week course at Inveraray was extremely tough and exacting. Those who fell by the wayside were immediately returned whence they had come. The right to wear Commando insignia was very hard earned and a source of immense pride to the wearers, as it is in the Royal Marines today – and rightly.

Understandably, there were many Commanding Officers in the Army who were deeply suspicious of what they saw as a piratical exercise that was creaming off all their best soldiers and officers. Some also saw the call for volunteers as a means of offloading some of their 'hard cases' and trouble makers. However, as William Seymour observes:

> *There is no place in Special Forces for scallywags in search of adventure ... but there is plenty of opportunity for men with courage, intelligence, initiative and self-discipline.*

These were the qualities the Commandos demanded and the 'pirates' were mostly weeded out in short order. Later, Seymour goes on:

Commandos undergoing training. Failure to match-up to the rigorous standards meant a return to unit.

Throughout the story of Special Forces ... the quality of courage runs as a golden thread through the rich tapestry of a colourful type of warfare.

The first major Commando raid, against the Lafoten Islands, off the north-west coast of Norway and within the Arctic Circle, was launched in March, 1941. The concept was brilliant, for the islands, which were of immense importance to the Germans as a source of vast quantities of fish oil, needed for the manufacture of nitro-glycerine for ammunition, were not heavily garrisoned or fortified. Provided the raid had been properly planned and rehearsed and surprise was achieved, there was every chance of an important success at a low cost.

The force consisted of some 500 men of Nos 3 and 4 Commandos, supported by 50 Royal Engineers and a similar number of Free Norwegian soldiers. Surprise was complete and the attack on the four islands created havoc. All the oil stocks were burned, the factories and other installations were destroyed and 20,000 tons of shipping were sunk. It was a bloodless affair, the only casualty being an officer who shot himself in the thigh with an accidental discharge! In addition to a substantial haul of prisoners, the Commandos came away with some 60 Norwegian Quislings and 315 Norwegian volunteers.

The Commandos had arrived. They had closed with the enemy and had shown what could be achieved by a small force of well-trained, well-led, determined men and the use of surprise. The world took note. By no means the least important aspect

South Vaagso on the south-western coast of Norway was successfully raided by British Commandos in December 1941.

Valuable stores going up in flames depriving the Germans of oil supplies.

German prisoners 'encouraged' to pose for the camera.

of the raid was the sterling support given by the Royal Navy, marking the beginning of an unbreakable bond with Commando Forces.

By the end of 1941, Keyes was beginning to show his age and was replaced by Lord Louis Mountbatten who at once set about creating a much larger and more elaborate Combined Operations Headquarters (COHQ) and getting his own position and status elevated so that he now became a Vice-Admiral, with comparable ranking in the other two Services, and a seat on the Chiefs of Staff Committee – the Lafoten Islands raid must have done much to make all that possible.

Hardly had Mountbatten assumed office then he launched the first of three large scale raids. This was against the small but heavily defended port of South Vaagso and the neighbouring island of Maaloy on the south-western coast of Norway. The Commando element of the force, some 600 men, included No 3 Commando and detachments from Nos 2, 4 and 6. Once again, there was also a contingent of Free Norwegians. The operation was to be heavily supported by both the Navy and the RAF.

Although surprise was again achieved, the German garrison of South Vaagso fought with great determination and there was bitter street fighting. However, the Commando offensive spirit and excellent training proved too much for the enemy. 120 Germans were killed and nearly 100 more taken prisoner. The Commandos lost 17 dead and 53 wounded. The damage done to the port and installations and to shipping in the harbour was extensive and the raid a great success. This marked a very important step forward for Special Forces for the Commandos had now proved that they could not only carry out a well planned operation but could outfight a determined enemy. The boost to public and Service morale was considerable. Furthermore, as had been hoped, the raid induced the Germans to increase their outlying garrisons.

The next raid, on the French naval port of St Nazaire, was what Montgomery would have called '*a real rough house*' and another resounding success, leading to the award of no less than five Victoria Crosses.

St Nazaire, at the mouth of the River Loire, possessed the largest dry dock in the world and was the last port left on the Atlantic coast which was capable of taking a German capital ship, such as the pocket battleships which were playing such an important part in the Battle of the Atlantic in 1942. It had become very important that the dock should be put out of action. It was therefore decided to ram the dock gates with the old American destroyer, HMS *Campbeltown* and to destroy as much of the dock installations as possible. She sailed under a strong naval escort and accompanied by just under 300 men from No 2 Commando, commanded by Lieutenant Colonel A.C. Newman, and demolition parties from 1,3,4,5,9 and 12 Commandos, all carried in motor launches (MLs). The force commander was Commander R.E.D. Ryder RN. The date, 27 March, 1942.

Once more, surprise was complete and the *Campbeltown* was well and truly jammed into the great lock gates before the Germans had any inkling of what was

The *Campbeltown* firmly wedged in the caisson of the Normandie dock at St Nazaire. The Germans remained unaware that the ship's bow was packed with explosives.

After the explosion, the shattered hulk resting in the Normandie dock.

afoot. However, they then reacted sharply and the defensive posts along the river began to engage the MLs, many of which were extensively damaged and a number of men killed. Nevertheless, those demolition parties that did get through managed to effect heavy damage within the port area. Having lost most of their craft by this time, a large number of Commandos were captured and fifty-nine killed, so that only just over one third of them returned. The Germans set about *Campbeltown* like a swarm of ants, little realizing that she was packed with explosives with time pencils set on delay. Some twelve hours after the initial attack, she blew up with devastating effect and killing a large number of the enemy at the same time. It should be remembered that it was almost exactly one month since the fall of Singapore and three since the loss of the *Prince of Wales* and the *Repulse*, public morale was low and the Navy suffering deeply from the loss of those two fine ships. The impact of this heroic triumph at St Nazaire at such a time was of immense importance. Once again, the Navy and Special Forces had carried the fight to the enemy with heartlifting results.

Mountbatten's third major raid was on quite a different scale from anything that had gone before. Two Canadian infantry brigades and a regiment of Churchill tanks were to assault the fortified port of Dieppe. Two Commandos would operate against the coastal artillery covering the port. The story of the tragic disaster which this operation became is too well known to repeat here. Suffice it to say that the Canadians had nearly seventy per cent casualties. What the operation did show was that any major invasion should be based upon the use of beaches rather than any form of port.

The blame for that disaster must be laid at the door of the Chief of Combined Operations for the raid was simply not properly planned or prepared. The Intelligence warnings were ignored. What is less well known is the stirring performance of the Commandos in their flanking operations to suppress the German batteries covering the assault area.

Nos 3 and 4 Commandos were each assigned a battery to neutralize. Unfortunately, 3 Commando was embarked in some unsuitable landing craft which were barely fit to attempt a Channel crossing and were unarmed. They were spotted and attacked by armed trawlers. The Commando was scattered and, in the end, only one party, of eighteen men under Major Peter Young, finally arrived at the correct beach. With great courage, they fought their way to the top of the high ground on which the battery was sited and kept up so heavy a fire upon the gun position that the guns could not be brought to bear upon the assault beach. On the Western flank, Lord Lovat's No 4 Commando, safely delivered under cover of darkness, put in a model attack and silenced their battery after a bayonet charge and fierce hand-to-hand fighting. The cost was forty-five casualties, of whom twelve were killed. The Germans lost thirty dead and as many again wounded. The operation took place on 18–19 August, 1942. It is of interest that a party from the 1st United States Rangers (their equivalent of the Commandos) accompanied each Commando on this occasion.

Aftermath of the disastrous raid on the fortified port of Dieppe where two Canadian infantry brigades were landed and suffered nearly seventy per cent casualties. It was claimed that valuable lessons were learned and saved lives when the Allies landed in Normandy in June 1944. One small party of No. 3 Commando carried out their unit's assigned task succesfully and with great gallantry. American Rangers went along for the experience.

Despite the chaos of Dieppe, from which the Commandos had emerged with a good deal of credit, it had by now been established, once and for all, that high quality troops, thoroughly trained and fearlessly led, with high morale and a well-developed offensive spirit, could achieve results out of all proportion to the strength of the force involved, given good planning and employment in their proper role. The early successes I have described here left no one in any doubt that Special Forces had come to stay.

Towards the end of 1942, Commando operations began to be mounted on a larger scale. Commando Brigades featured in planning of major amphibious operations and even, in North West Europe, when manpower was getting short in 1944–45, in the land battles. Nevertheless, both in the Mediterranean and the Far East, many smaller scale operations were very successful and the Special Boat Section (SBS) did sterling work in both areas, often in co-operation with forces controlled by the Special Operations Executive (SOE).

The Commando scene had expanded considerably when nine Royal Marine Commandos were formed from the Royal Marine Division. The men were not volunteers and had not been through the Commando Training Centre at that stage. This led to some tension between the old hands and the newcomers, as it was felt that they were 'horning in' on the Army's act. This situation needed firm and tactful handling for it was unhelpful and not to be accepted. Fortunately some shrewd and sensible measures, such as cross posting of carefully selected officers together with the shared experience of some hard and successful fighting, soon created the right bond of comradeship and a shared cause. Perhaps the most notable of these shared operations was the breaching of the defences of the island of Walcheren in November, 1944, which opened the Scheldt estuary and gave access to the vital port of Antwerp.

It was a sad time when the Army Commandos were disbanded, together with all the other Special Forces at the end of the war, but, happily, the role stayed with the Royal Marines, in whose safe hands it has gone from strength to strength.

Whilst the Commandos were expanding and developing their skills and expertise through the invaluable experience of active operations, new Special Forces were springing up in the Middle East.

* * *

General Sir Archibald Wavell, the Commander-in-Chief, was a man with an uncanny grasp of the nature of war. He was always ready to support any innovation which he felt made military sense and would pay a worthwhile dividend. Thus it comes as no surprise to find that it was he, rather than a disbelieving staff, who responded to the imaginative ideas of Major Ralph Bagnold, an officer in the Royal Signals who had made a name for himself as an adventurous explorer of the Libyan Desert, just before the outbreak of war. With a number of kindred spirits, Bagnold had shown that the sand seas of the desert, believed by most people to be impassable to vehicles, could be traversed, given the right type of truck, the necessary know-how, navigating skills and equipment. This was a man after Wavell's own heart.

It is not generally realized that the Libyan Desert covers a land mass nearly the size of India. Hence, any form of mobile warfare across its face involves huge mileages, considerable dispersion and inevitable vulnerability, for such key features as supply dumps, airfields and ports, to surprise attack. Furthermore all routine movement of troops and logistic traffic is inescapably tied to the few proper roads or the railways. Clearly, as Bagnold had suggested to Wavell, there was considerable scope for a clandestine group, moving well behind the enemy's forward areas, not only to harass him but, by careful surveillance from concealed positions, to obtain priceless information on enemy movement. Wavell was convinced and agreed.

Given the go-ahead and virtual *carte blanche*, Bagnold at once began to gather up men and material for what was to become known as the Long Range Desert Group (LRDG). He was lucky enough to get 100 men and two officers from the New Zealanders for a start. Other sources, the Guards, the Canadians, the Yeomanry all produced high class men and officers attracted by the sound of the project. With some difficulty, a fleet of 30 cwt Chevrolet trucks was acquired and by 5 August, 1940, training was ready to begin.

The main task of the LRDG would be reconnaissance but they would hope to bring in '*a prisoner or two*' and to do what damage they could without hazarding their principal role. They planned on patrols lasting three weeks, each covering about 2,000 miles – a very tough commitment and one that called for the highest standards of navigation. Bagnold himself, working on the original sun-compasses produced by the desert patrols of the First World War, produced an excellent new compass in conjunction with a young officer of the 1st Royal Tank Regiment, Rae Leakey. He also developed a system of condensers for the vehicles' radiators to enable them to compete with the immense heat and slogging going that they would have to face, week after week.

Their initial training completed, Bagnold soon moved his squadrons forward to the two oases of Kufra and Siwa from where they operated until Rommel's final advance after the Battle of Gazala in 1942.

Bagnold's Second-in-Command was Major Guy Prendergast of the Royal Tank Regiment, an experienced desert traveller and a fine pilot. When Bagnold was promoted and moved to a staff job at General Headquarters, Prendergast succeeded him in command and at once acquired two light aircraft, one of which he piloted and maintained himself, the other being flown by a trooper who was also an experienced pilot. Those machines would prove invaluable in many ways, including emergency casualty evacuation.

The glorious story of the LRDG is superbly described by Major General David Lloyd Owen in his *Providence Their Guide* (recently republished by Leo Cooper, Pen & Sword Books). One of the original officers of the Group and its Commanding

Workhorse of the Long Range Desert Group, the Chevrolet 30 cwt. This crew is having a 'brew-up' and resting in the shade of their vehicle.

The enemy airfield at Barce after a visit from the Long Range Desert Group.

Officer for the last two years of the war, he was the ideal man to write its history. There is no space to relate that story here but suffice it to say that the LRDG became not only a rich source of invaluable intelligence through its surveillance of enemy movement (known as 'road watching') but a thorn in the enemy's side, as it worked hand in hand with the Special Air Service, as described below.

Like the Commandos, the LRDG proved, time and again, that training, skill, fortitude, courage, determination and the use of surprise, enabled small groups of fighting men to be a severe source of embarrassment to the enemy and to pay dividends out of all proportion to their size. Once the desert war was over and the fighting spread to Tunisia, which was not suitable for the LRDG's type of operations, they developed new skills and tactics to play a very significant role within the Mediterranean Theatre, from the Greek Islands to the Adriatic.

The war over, David Lloyd Owen fought hard to get the LRDG kept in the Order of Battle of the peacetime Army – but to no avail.

Whilst the principal mission of the LRDG in the desert was reconnaissance, with offensive operations taking second place, the Special Air Service, whose origins date from the early summer of 1941, was essentially a raiding organization but, because it lacked its own means of mobility, it depended heavily upon the LRDG for its movement. Thus the two were very closely linked.

After the fall of Crete in May, 1941, a number of officers in 8 Commando, part of a group commanded by Colonel R.E. Laycock, who would later become Chief of Combined Operations, were feeling very much as they had after Dunkirk – that there was an urgent need to get at the Germans.

With time hanging rather heavy on their hands, they thought of parachuting as a possible new skill by means of which they might achieve their laudable aim. With Laycock's encouragement, they acquired some parachutes and the use of a suitable aircraft and made their first jump. There was only one casualty, David Stirling, an officer of the Scots Guards, whose chute malfunctioned, landing him in hospital for several weeks. As he lay there, Stirling's imaginative mind and unquenchable love of adventure led his thoughts to the possibility of mounting deep penetration raids, involving the use of parachutes, by small patrols of highly trained, determined men capable of using their own initiative and judgement. A man of great personality and determination, to whom obstacles only existed to be demolished, Stirling persuaded General Auchinleck, then the Commander-in-Chief, to allow him to recruit and train such a unit with an initial strength of sixty-five men and a Bombay aircraft from which to jump.

Although originally designated 62 Commando, Stirling's new force was soon known as the Special Air Service (SAS). His team included a number of men whose gallantry and fighting qualities would make them a legend in the story of Special Forces. Chief of these was Captain Paddy Mayne who, by the end of the war, would be commanding the 1st SAS Regiment and have won no less than four DSOs. Like Stirling, he lived to destroy all things German.

David Stirling.

Paddy Mayne.

David Stirling's first raid, which took place in November, 1941, and involved a drop by fifty-five men, was a disaster. The weather was foul and few of the men landed anywhere near the objective. Bitterly disappointed, Stirling took this set-back as a signal to redouble his efforts and to get on with planning a series of raids for December.

However, he did realise that unless he was going to risk another failure, he must get the LRDG, who had recovered what was left of the first shambles and brought them back in safety, to act as a taxi service. Despite the burden which this placed upon them, the LRDG responded magnificently and a close comradeship soon bonded these two fine fighting forces.

The December raids against the Germans' forward airfields were a stunning success and the future of the SAS was secured. Not long after, during a visit to Cairo of the Prime Minister, whose sense of the heroic made him a wholehearted supporter of what David Stirling was doing, the SAS became officially recognized as a regiment of the regular Army on the Order of Battle.

The Regiment went from strength to strength. In the middle of 1942, they acquired their own Jeeps, now made available through Lease Lend by the Americans. With one jeep per four man patrol, each vehicle carrying twin Vickers 'K' machine-guns (which had a tremendous rate of fire) and some mounting .50 Browning guns in addition, the whole character of their operations changed, thanks to their new-found mobility and fire power. Though still in close touch with the LRDG, the latter had been eased of a considerable burden.

Stirling soon worked out his ideas on the tactical use of these new assets and, in a raid against Landing Field 12 at Sidi Haneish, he used no less than eighteen jeeps, first in extended line and then in double line ahead, with all guns

The right vehicle for the Special Air Service, the GPW (General Purpose Willys) better known as the Jeep, with twin Vickers K machine guns and a Browning machine gun.

blazing. Over thirty aircraft were destroyed at the cost of three jeeps. In the midst of the inferno they had created, and because of the need to disperse after the attack had been made, the exact number of planes knocked out was never known. Seymour describes the raid as '*a magnificent mounted manoeuvre performed to perfection*'.

In February, 1943, during operations in Tunisia, David Stirling was captured. Erwin Romel was amongst those who realized the loss to the British that Stirling's capture meant and, of course, what, hopefully, it would mean to his own army and air forces.

The impact of Stirling's departure from the scene was, in fact, far greater than was at first realized, for he was a man who committed very little to paper and carried his plans and administrative data mainly in his head, so that even his adjutant was seldom 'in the know'. There was nothing for it but to start all over again and organize a new regiment. Two new squadrons were now formed, the Special Raiding Squadron under Paddy Mayne and the Special Boat Squadron under Lord Jellicoe. Lieutenant Colonel Cator, late of 51 Commando, took command. Although the new organization was initially known as Raiding Forces, it was not long before Cator restored its proper name and it became the 1st SAS Regiment – and rightly. Meanwhile, David Stirling's elder brother Bill had formed a second regiment. Later there would be an SAS Brigade, which would contain some Allied elements.

Like the LRDG, the SAS now became heavily involved in the fighting in and around Greece and Yugoslavia. Later they would achieve great things in highly secret operations in North-West Europe. There is no doubt that the LRDG and SAS had truly demonstrated the art of deep penetration and had '*engaged the enemy more closely*'. They had also proved, beyond any shadow of doubt, the power of the small, heavily armed mobile patrol manned by well-trained, determined, fit and resourceful men.

By the end of the fighting in the Libyan Desert, the SAS had accounted for nearly 400 enemy aircraft and left a blazing trail of wrecked supply dumps, port installations and airfields and a substantial number of German and Italian dead. From then on, the activities of the SAS intensified and spread as the size of the Regiment increased. Today, the resurrected SAS is the envy of armies throughout the world.

* * *

Before we turn to the roles and activities of the highly secret SOE, we must first pay a tribute to the part played in the Middle East and Mediterranean Theatres by another remarkable raiding force, Popski's Private Army and its heroic commander, Colonel Vladimir Peniakoff.

'Popski' as he was christened by the LRDG, who found Peniakoff too much of a mouthful, was a Russian refugee who had left Belgium, where he was studying engineering and mathematics in the University of Brussels on the outbreak of war in 1914. Coming to England, he went to Cambridge but left without a degree and by 1939 was working in Egypt as an engineer in a French sugar company. In 1939 he returned to England to fight for Britain, which he had learned to love and admire over the years. Somehow, he managed to acquire a commission on the General List in the Libyan Arab Force (LAF) but soon found the job dull and frustrating. Thanks, no doubt, to his own lobbying, in March, 1942, he found himself appointed to command a detachment of the LAF designated as the Libyan Arab Force Commando with a mission to collect and collate intelligence on the enemy's movements in the area of the Jebel Akhdar. His little Commando consisted of an Arab Officer, a British Sergeant and twenty-two Senussi from the LAF. For mobility, he was dependent upon the LRDG, who admired his dash and guts but found that his unfamiliarity with time and the truth tended to make him a tiresome bed-fellow. Nevertheless, he and his men learned much from them and, thanks to them, were able to carry out most of the tasks being undertaken by the two main raiding forces – intelligence gathering, the destruction of petrol dumps and aircraft and so on. However, the trouble with Popski, in the eyes of the professionals, was that he was too 'slap happy' in his planning and although he had many successes, too many operations failed, Seymour tells us, 'through lack of sound administration' and, as an officer of the LRDG put it, through 'being planned in a carefree Boy Scout manner'. So it comes as no surprise to find that when Popski suggested that his little force should form a squadron of the LRDG the idea was rejected. However, that great soldier, Shan Hackett, then a Colonel responsible for all raiding forces in the Middle East, decided that Popski had the makings of a commander of a motorized raiding group, so No 1 Demolition Squadron was born. The title was too unglamorous for Popski, who called it Popski's Private Army (PPA) and the name stuck, even to the extent of having PPA added to the original, formal title!

Popski at the wheel of his jeep, somewhere in Italy, with Bob Park-Yunnie standing.

Lieutenant Colonel Vladimir Peniakoff.

The story of the adventures of the PPA reads more like that of war fiction than the fact that it was. Mounted in jeeps, bristling with medium and heavy machine-guns and carrying a number of 3″ mortars, the small group, never more than 100 strong and often less than half that number, harassed the enemy in Tunisia and Italy right up to the end of the war, sometimes alone and sometimes in co-operation with other troops. In northern Italy they worked very successfully with the Italian Partisans. It cannot be said that the PPA had a significant impact on the outcome of the campaigns within which they fought but they were unquestionably a real thorn in the side of the enemy.

Popski managed to recruit some wonderful characters and was blessed with two extremely good and brave officers, Jean Caneri, a Free Frenchman from Syria and a Scots Captain from the LAF, Bob Park-Yunnie, described by Seymour as '*second only to Popski, perhaps the most remarkable man who served in the PPA… a born leader, a skilful and courageous fighter with a keen, incisive mind and resilient spirit*'. Although he eventually had four further officers, Popski owed much of his success to the stalwart support of those two, his sheet anchors.

Despite the rather piratical nature of the PPA, the standard of training, mostly under Yunnie, was extremely high, tough and demanding. Each man, in addition to being '*a highly skilled driver, had to be a good machine-gunner, mechanic and demolition expert*'. Popski's insistence upon those standards was unyielding. He saw the Army as a 'Band of Brothers', close knit by constant danger and tempered by friendship. Their story ended on a high note. Between 21 and 30 April, 1945, they took 1,335 prisoners, 16 field guns and countless smaller weapons. Popski had lost a hand in the gallant rescue of two isolated dismounted troops of the 27th Lancers and had won a well-earned DSO.

* * *

We have now seen something of the story of the development of Special Forces from the aftermath of Dunkirk to the end of the war in Europe and, hopefully, the reader will have got some idea of what Special Forces were and what part they played in the overall conduct of the war. It is to be hoped too that the quality, courage and comradeship which characterized them has also come through. However, there was an immensely important organization, the Special Operations Executive (SOE) which, whilst not strictly matching the definition on page 153 must be seen as an historic and deeply significant element of what the man in the street rightly thinks of when the term Special Forces is used.

SOE was an early by product of Churchill's stirring directive, issued in July, 1941, to '*set Europe alight*'. Essentially, SOE was the controlling authority for all operations in enemy occupied territory and so a very secret, clandestine organization. As we have already seen, the only exception to that authority was the SAS, who declined to operate under people who had no first hand knowledge of their work.

By its very nature, this was an organization that worked in small groups though often co-ordinating the activities of several larger groups of local resistance forces. Thus, essentially, its people were agents who helped, trained and advised those forces. They also oversaw the working of the escape routes for Allied prisoners and fellow agents on the run. Working mostly in pairs of a leader and his wireless operator, they kept in touch with London and transmitted SOE's instructions to local leaders. In addition, they were often involved in the reception of arms and new agents. They seldom actually commanded but their influence with the resistance fighters was, of course, considerable. As far as is known, only one British officer, Captain Michel Trotobas, a former staff sergeant in the Middlesex Regiment, who was half French, actually commanded a *Reseau* (or fighting group) of the Maquis (as the French resistance movement was known). Of legendary courage and daring, the date of his death in a shoot out with the Gestapo is still remembered annually in Lille, the centre of his operations.

The influence of SOE quickly spread across the face of Europe, in the Mediterranean and in Yugoslavia, where its agents worked closely with the SAS and LRDG.

Britain had an extensive refugee population, mostly from Nazi domination and there were many brave men and women who were prepared to face the awful risks inherent in an agent's life. Today it is not easy for us to appreciate fully the measure of the stress they underwent in the face of the combined threats of a very aggressive, ruthless and vigilant Gestapo, aided and abetted by the local police, and treachery on the part of their fellow countrymen and women. In France alone, no less than 200 SOE agents were captured and tortured by the Gestapo. Only thirty survived. Their cold blooded heroism and their conduct under torture are a golden page in the history of Special Forces.

All too little is known, even now, about the scale of naval and air support given to the SOE but it was massive and almost all was very hazardous. Without it, SOE could not have survived. The BBC too played a vital role by transmitting coded messages to the resistance organizations in their news bulletins to the occupied countries, bulletins which meant so much to the people who daily risked their lives to get the only truthful information about the progress of the war which was available.

Major General Colin Gubbins.

Because its operations were primarily land based, SOE had a preponderance of soldiers running the organization. Their Head was Major General Colin Gubbins, who, as a Lieutenant Colonel, led those five Independent Companies to Norway in 1940. Most of the agents were dressed as General List officers although there were certainly some airmen and sailors and members of the Women's Services amongst them who were appropriately dressed. For ever to be associated with SOE was the First Aid Nursing Yeomanry (the FANYs) who not only produced a number of agents but formed several vitally important wireless units who worked to the agents and military missions run by SOE, thereby making a crucially important contribution to the success of its operations.

In England, SOE's nerve centre was in London in secure houses whilst the agents were held and trained mainly in isolated country houses where secrecy and security could be more easily maintained. From these bases, some were ferried to airfields from where they would be flown to parachute dropping zones or delivered, by brave RAF pilots in Lysander aircraft, to secret landing strips. The local resistance movement would arrange the meetings – unless the Gestapo got there first. Others were taken to beaches where they would board submarines and move in by sea.

A Halifax MkII, 138 Squadron at RAF Tempsford. Agents were parachuted into enemy-held territory and supplies dropped to the Resistance from this field. A barn on the edge of the airfield, used during the war by agents awaiting their aircraft, still stands as a memorial to those who took off from there and subsequently lost their lives.

In the Far East, SOE set up various 'Forces', of which Force 136 was the largest and most important, all involved in the promotion of guerrilla warfare in Japanese occupied territory and the gathering of intelligence. In Burma, Force 136 worked close behind the Japanese lines, chiefly to acquire intelligence but also to harass the enemy when this was possible. In Malaya, Force 136 was involved in the support of an organization known as the Malayan People's Anti-Japanese Army, raised by the Malayan Communist Party under whose control it operated. It was a sad quirk of fate that this should have been the shadow behind the Malayan Emergency in the 1950s, many of the terrorists involved being former members and bearing arms and equipment supplied to them by SOE during the war. Unlike the lowland Burmese, who were dominated by the Japanese, the Naga and Karen hillmen from the Burmese borders were anxious to fight them and to ensure the safety of their villages. A number fought with Force 136 and other SOE organizations, to whom their brave support and local knowledge were invaluable.

It was not until 1943 that the American counterpart to SOE, the Office of Strategic Studies (OSS), was ready for operations. As Peter Taylor describes on page 179, the OSS was raised and directed by Colonel William Donovan who had, until 1942, been working with SOE. William Stephenson, a Canadian, stationed in New York, who was a close friend of Winston Churchill, co-ordinated the work of SOE, the British Security Services and OSS with Donovan. The work of OSS was somewhat circumscribed by two factors. The first, rather surprisingly, was that the Americans found themselves unable to produce agents capable of passing themselves off as 'locals' in the countries of Europe as was done by SOE. The second was that General MacArthur had forbidden the presence of OSS in his Southwest Pacific Command. In consequence, its activities were very largely confined to North-West Africa, Burma and China, with the notable exception of an organization known as the Jedburghs in which they worked with SOE. The Jedburghs consisted of small parties fed, initially, into France to help co-ordinate resistance operations against the Germans during the run-up period to D-Day (June 1944). Later they would operate in Burma and China. Some Jedburghs were also deployed in Operation MARKET GARDEN (Nijmegen and Arnhem) in September, 1944, to work with the Dutch. Finally, OSS was involved in a short-lived organization called the Special Allied Airborne Reconnaissance Force which, as Taylor says, was disbanded after only seven weeks. Some American Jedburghs were incorporated in it.

Major General Orde Wingate.

OSS ran a successful espionage ring in Switzerland. Its head, Allen Dulles, played an important part in the negotiations for the German surrender in Italy in April, 1945.

* * *

In February, 1943, a mixed force of volunteers from many different units, including a number of Commandos from England, with varying experience, was raised in India under the title of 77th (Indian) Brigade (The Chindits). The man behind this move was Brigadier Orde Wingate, a most unorthodox and eccentric officer but an experienced guerrilla fighter, having led a clandestine force, known as the Special Night Squads, in Palestine in 1936 and his very successful Gideon Force in Ethiopia in 1940, with which he had harassed the Italians and captured a number of their forts. Deeply depressed in England, where he had been on the staff, he proposed to General Wavell, the Commander-in-Chief in India, that he should lead a deep penetration operation into Burma. Wavell, being very familiar with his work with Gideon, and always attracted by new ideas, at once agreed and Operation LONGCLOTH was launched. In February, 1943, 77 Brigade, divided into six 'columns', two to each battalion, marched in across the Chindwin, every officer and man, regardless of rank, carrying a load of 70lbs on his back. The actual damage done by the operation was rather limited and the columns seem to have wandered rather aimlessly, incurring a number of casualties in the process, but nevertheless, making the Japanese acutely aware of a vulnerability of which they had not previously been conscious. Despite the high casualty rate incurred by *77* Brigade, the powers that be fell in with Wingate's suggestion that a much more substantial force should be raised to establish a positive presence in the depths of the jungle from where it

Imphal, February 1943, Wavell bids farewell to one of the groups about to set off into Burma on operation LONGCLOTH.

would harass the Japanese lines of communication and create mayhem in the rear areas, forcing the enemy to deploy a large number of troops to counter its activities. This was, of course, just the sort of adventurous operation that appealed to Winston Churchill and he backed Wingate, now a Major General to the hilt.

No less than 20,000 men, in six brigades, were formed into the Special Force. Whilst LONGCLOTH had been supplied by air, the intention was that Operation THURSDAY, as it was to be called, should not only be supplied by air but that much of the force would be flown in to prepared strips in association with which heavily fortified jungle strongpoints would be established. It was launched in March, 1944.

Unlike LONGCLOTH, it was to be a much more conventional operation with all the supporting arms of an infantry division and a mass of mules to carry the heavy weapons and ammunition of the mobile columns.

This was not a voluntary affair. As Peter Taylor shows on pages 84–85 the brigades consisted chiefly of units taken from the regular order of battle, any weak links having been combed out during the intensive preliminary training period. Once the columns began to destroy rail communications, fuel dumps and the like, the Japanese reacted strongly and casualties soon began to mount. Unlike LONGCLOTH, in which a merciful bullet was often the only answer to a serious wound, on THURSDAY it was often possible to fly casualties out.

Wingate was killed in an air crash fairly early on and Brigadier Joe Lentaigne, a much more conventional officer, took over. Despite some valuable successes, the operation as a whole must be seen as something of a failure. The cost in effort had been prodigious and the price paid in human lives was high. One might almost say that the principal lesson that emerged was the courage and fortitude of the ordinary British, Indian and African soldiers who took part, showing that, given the training, they did not have to be supermen to cope with the demands put upon them or to match the Japanese in a jungle fight. It was the first Allied operation to use air power on such a scale and the logistical and technical experience gained was certainly extremely valuable.

Though unconventional in concept, the scale and the conventional nature of the force employed for Operation THURSDAY were such that it is hard to reconcile it with the concept of Special Forces.

* * *

Airborne Forces had long been established as an integral part of both German and Russian forces so it might well be argued that they hardly qualified for the title of Special Forces either. However, the British airborne forces did have their roots in the Army Commandos and No 2 Commando became the 1st Battalion of the Parachute Regiment. Though the first ever British parachute operation was a rather abortive affair in Italy, William Seymour describes the second one, the Bruneval raid, in February, 1942, against a German Wurzburg radar station in northern France, led by Major John Frost (later to be the hero of Arnhem), as '*the most successful and least*

German prisoners captured during the Bruneval raid. One was a radar technician who was most helpful.

Major John Frost on board the *Prinz Albert* after the raid.

costly raid undertaken by components of all three Services'. Under Frost, C Company of the 2nd Battalion of the Parachute Regiment seized the radar site, killed thirty Germans and got away with all the technical equipment they had been tasked to recover. They even brought home three prisoners! A masterpiece of good planning and high class training.

Although the parachutists were all volunteers, the units of the air landing brigades in the two British Airborne Divisions were all units from the regular order of battle. Of all the members of the Airborne Forces, perhaps the Glider Pilot Regiment are most deserving of the Special Forces cachet. Not only did they fly the heavy gliders which brought in the airlanding brigades and some other elements of the divisions but, once they had landed, they became highly trained fighting men giving support where required. At Arnhem they really proved their worth and a number paid with their lives.

* * *

Generally speaking, the American Raiders, Rangers and Airborne Forces, all magnificent troops, were trained on British lines. Led by some inspiring commanders, all made great names for themselves as doughty fighters, as of course, did the United States Marines with whom the Raiders and Rangers fought in the Pacific in some of the toughest and bloodiest fighting of the Second World War.

* * *

Glider pilots under instruction. Their task was to land the troops and equipment in their charge safely, then fight alongside the airborne troops.

Troops of the US 17th Airborne Division passing through the town of Appelnhulsen, Germany, on their way to the City of Munster in the spring of 1945.

It was understandable that the early misgivings expressed about the creation of 'Private Armies' should have tended to live on throughout much of the war. Hard pressed commanders trying to build up formations for operations, often with limited resources, must have been very frustrated to see their best men and equipment which they needed, being diverted. Furthermore, when operations like THURSDAY were launched on so large a scale for what even General Bill Slim saw as questionable advantage, eyebrows were bound to have been raised. It should be recognized that most Special Forces operations were clandestine and it was not until their stories began to be written in the post-war period that we really began to appreciate the measure of their achievements. Those who fought alongside the Commando Brigades in North-West Europe had no doubt about their quality or about the value of the service they gave. The LRDG and SAS, both relatively small organizations, often working in small packets, rendered service out of all proportion to their size.

If, as Peter Taylor tells us, the insignia described in this book were worn with great pride, history has shown us that the wearers had every reason to do so.

Bryan Watkins

Chapter 1

Combined Operations

Not until 1937 was any action taken to study and coordinate inter-service exercises and operations. A committee was set up by the War Office to examine the problems and a year later, the Inter-Services Training and Development Centre (later to become the Combined Operations Training Centre) was established near Portsmouth. As part of his determination '*to set Europe alight*' Winston Churchill initiated the establishment of a Combined Operations Headquarters. This was initially part of the Admiralty under Admiral Sir Roger Keyes as Director. In 1941, Vice-Admiral Lord Louis Mountbatten became Chief of Combined Operations with a separate headquarters and a much bigger staff. He had a seat on the Chiefs of Staff Committee and responsibility for all aspects of Commando training and operations. His headquarters (COHQ) now became the mounting authority for all raiding against North-West Europe. (Combined Operations insignia are on pages 34 and 63.)

The Army Commando

In 1940, on the orders of the War Office, twelve Commando battalions and ten Independent Companies were to be raised. The Independent Companies were raised from the following divisions:

No 1 Company from 52nd Lowland Division.
No 2 Company from 53rd Welsh Division.
No 3 Company from 54th East Anglian Division.
No 4 Company from 55th West Lancashire Division.
No 5 Company from 56th (1st London) Division.
No 6 Company from 9th Scottish Division.
No 7 Company from 15th Scottish Division.
No 8 Company from 18th Eastern Division.
No 9 Company from 38th Welsh Division.
No 10 Company from 66th East Lancashire Division.

It is known that only No 4 Company of the 55th West Lancashire Division wore its own patch, the 55th Division patch, consisting of a rose on which was superimposed the figure '4' in red stitching.

The Commandos were raised from the following commands: No 2 Commando was raised as a parachute unit with volunteers from all commands. Numbers 3 and 4 Commandos from Southern Command. Numbers 5 and 6 Commandos from Western Command. No 7 Commando from Eastern Command. No 8 Commando from Eastern Command but actually raised from the London district and Household Division. Numbers 9 and 11 Commandos from Scottish Command. No 10 Commando was formed from Northern Command but they were unable to raise sufficient volunteers and it was disbanded in December 1940. It was reformed in 1942. No 12 Commando was raised from men stationed in Northern Ireland.

In October, 1940, the Independent Companies and Commando Battalion were formed into a Special Service (SS) Brigade. It was raised from the following:

1st SS BN formed from 1, 2, 3, 4, 5, 8 and 9 Independent Companies.
2nd SS BN formed from Nos. 6 and 7 Independent Companies and Nos. 9 and 11 Commandos.

3rd SS BN formed from Nos. 4 and 7 Commandos.
4th SS BN formed from Nos. 3 and 8 Commandos.
5th SS BN formed from Nos. 5 and 6 Commandos.

No 2 Commando became 11 Special Air Service Battalion and eventually became 1st Parachute Battalion. No 12 Commando remained outside the Special Service Brigade and stayed in Northern Ireland. They wore no shoulder title but some of the Service Battalion wore shoulder patches.

The second SS Battalion wore crossed green claymores on a purple square.

HQ Company of the Brigade wore an oblong patch with two fighting knives in white with red S hilts. This also comes in bullion. HQ Signals wore an oblong patch with a knife facing upwards and a bolt of lightning running through and SS at each side. The knife and lightning were in white and the SS in red on a black background.

In March, 1941, the Special Service Brigade was disbanded and the battalion were to form the following:

No 1 Commando formed from 1 SS Battalion
No 2 Commando formed from 1 SS Battalion
No 3 Commando formed from 4 SS Battalion
No 4 Commando formed from 3 SS Battalion
No 5 Commando formed from 5 SS Battalion
No 6 Commando formed from 5 SS Battalion
No 7 Commando formed from 3 SS Battalion
No 8 Commando formed from 4 SS Battalion
No 9 Commando formed from 2 SS Battalion
No 11 Commando formed from 2 SS Battalion
No 12 Commando

All twelve Commando Battalions were disbanded by 1945.

Lofoten Raiding Party – No. 4 Troop. March, 1941.

No 1 Commando

Created from A Company 1st SS Battalion in March, 1941. The first shoulder title was 1 over COMMANDO in green on khaki and this changed early in 1943 to No 1 COMMANDO in red on dark blue. This title is found in woven or printed variations. 1 Commando wore a green salamander in a red and yellow flame on a khaki background below the shoulder title. 1941–1943 only. From 1943 it changed to the Combined Operations patch, red on dark blue.

Landing exercises in Scotland. This was on the occasion of King George VI's visit to the Commando training area.

Commandos crossing the Seine at Duclair, September, 1944.

Combined Operations patches. (Also see page 63)

No 2 Commando

Created from B Company 1st SS Battalion in March 1941, this unit was unique in that it was the only Commando unit to wear its own badge. The badge was a commando dagger with SS on the hilt in silver bullion on a black background or hand-made from canteen cutlery and was worn on a black patch. Officers wore the bullion version only.

Lieutenant Colonel Todd.

Officers of No 2 Commando wearing the metal cap badge.

The other ranks' badge was just the Commando dagger with no SS on the hilt. The first few were made by the men from canteen cutlery and then commercially made later on. Then, in late 1944 or early 1945 there appeared a cast brass version of the badge but nobody knows why this version was made. All the badges were worn on a black patch on their headgear. The first shoulder title was 2 COMMANDO white on black and in early 1943 changed to No 2 COMMANDO red on black; this variation is found in printed or woven examples.

The shoulder patch was a Commando dagger with SS on the hilt and was the same as the officer's cap badge. This was worn by all ranks. The patch was worn in pairs and appears in silver bullion wire and woven silk thread on a black oblong patch. The silver bullion was worn on the service dress uniform and the silk thread was worn on the battle dress. This patch disappeared in late 1943.

No 3 Commando

3 Commando was the first Commando unit to be formed in 1940. Up to 1941 they had no shoulder titles but wore individual troop patches. D Troop wore a white full-face death's head in a blue D on a dark green background. In mid-1941 the troops changed from letters to numbers which were 1 to 6 and HQ.

D troop became no 3 Troop but still wore the same patch and other troops wore patches as well. No 4 Troop wore a white death's head on a black disc and No 5 wore just a black disc. It is not known if other troops wore patches.

D Troop.   No. 3 Troop.

At the same time the new shoulder title 3 COMMANDO, white on black, appeared with the troop numbers underneath. HQ wore just 3 COMMANDO. In early 1943 a new title No 3 COMMANDO was introduced. This had no numbers beneath and was red on black and appeared in printed or woven form.

No 4 Commando

No 4 Commando was formed in mid-1940. The first shoulder title to be worn by them was SPECIAL IV SERVICE in white letters and salmon-pink Roman numerals on black. In 1941 this was changed to 4 COMMANDO with red number and light blue letters on black. In late 1942 they changed again to No 4 COMMANDO, red on black, printed or woven, also red on khaki. In 1940 when the unit was formed, only officers wore a silver cracked skull badge. It is not known why this badge was worn or how many were made.

In August 1942 three troops of French marines were added to the unit. The marines wore their own special badge and title. The first badge to be worn was a cap band in black with F N F L in gold letters. This was worn on the naval bonnet. On

SPECIAL IV SERVICE

4. COMMANDO

Nº4 COMMANDO

Nº4 COMMANDO

FRANCE

F.F. COMMANDO

the sleeves was FRANCE in large or small letters in white on khaki or white on navy blue. This was worn above the FF COMMANDO in red on black at first and then 4 COMMANDO in red on black. At the same time below the shoulder title they wore the F N F L patch which was a red cross of Lorraine in a white diamond on a blue shield with a yellow or white border (see page 48). In late 1942 when the troops got the beret, the sleeve patch was sewn on as a cap badge and in early 1944 a new metal badge was introduced. This was made at first by a local blacksmith in light-coloured bronze and numbered on the back, later by J. R. Gaunt in die-struck bronze. The badge was a shield with a cross of Lorraine in the top corner and a commando dagger going through a sailing ship. Beneath the shield was a scroll with 1st Bn FM COMMANDO.

No 5 Commando

Formed in the mid 1940s as A Company, 5th Special Service Battalion, the 5th wore no title but wore a golden coloured hackle in the beret. Because it was so fragile and easily got lost, it was discontinued by 1942.

The first shoulder title appeared when it separated from the Special Service Battalion in 1941 to become 5 Commando. This was V COMMANDO, gold on dark green. Sometime in mid 1942 the title 5 COMMANDO appeared. This was yellow gold on dark green. In early 1943 the title changed to No 5 COMMANDO, red on black in printed or woven variations. By the end of the war a brass shoulder title was being worn in the Far East – 5 over COMMANDO. Before 1943, 5 Commando wore a shoulder patch which was a V between two crossed daggers, all in yellow with black details on a green rectangular patch woven in silk.

No 6 Commando

This was formed in mid-1940 and then became B Company Special Service Battalion and in March 1941 reverted to its original title. The first shoulder title was VI COMMANDO, white on black and was changed in late 1942 to a white VI and COMMANDO in red and then in 1943 to No 6 COMMANDO, red on dark blue, in printed and woven variations. On the side cap they wore VI over COMMANDO, white on a black rectangle. They also wore just the VI in metal which was cut out of aluminium cans and stitched on to a black rectangle and a woven variation which was hand-made with white silk thread on a black oblong patch.

Within 6 COMMANDO, was a seaborne troop which used canoes or folding boats. This troop was called 101 Troop and had its own special patch worn in facing pairs below the shoulder title. This was a blue rectangle with a red 101 with a white swordfish emerging through the O, and came in printed and woven variations. 101 Troop were disbanded in early 1943 but the men helped to form the Special Boat Squadron.

Note VI over COMMANDO on side cap and arm. He is in US army uniform, May, 1943.

Military Medal winner of 101 Troop, 1942. Note VI over COMMANDO on shoulder.

No 7 Commando

This was formed in July 1940 and then became 2nd Special Service Company of the 3rd Special Service Battalion. On the disbandment of the Special Service Brigade in 1941 it was re-designated A Battalion of LAYFORCE. It is not known why the shoulder title No 7 COMMANDO, red on dark blue, was made in early 1943, but never worn.

No 8 Commando

This was formed in mid-1940 and then became B Company, 4th Special Service Battalion but suffered the same fate as 7 Commando by becoming B Battalion of LAYFORCE. It is not known why the shoulder title No 8 COMMANDO, red on dark blue was made in early 1943, but never worn.

No 9 Commando

Formed in mid 1940, it became A Company of the 2nd Special Service Battalion. As A Company they wore no titles but wore a black feather hackle in a khaki Balmoral hat; no cap badge was worn. In March 1941 they reverted to 9 COMMANDO but carried on wearing the khaki Balmoral and black hackle. In 1942 when they got their

green beret, they transferred the black hackle to it. The first known shoulder title was 9 COMMANDO, white on black. This was changed to No 9 COMMANDO, white on black, in late 1942.

Between late 1942 and early 1943 the shoulder title went through a number of changes. The first was No 9 COMMANDO, green on black, and then No 9 COMMANDO, red on black. This appears in woven and printed examples. Finally they went back to 9 COMMANDO, white on black. It is not known why they changed the title so often in this period.

No 10 Commando
This was formed in 1940 but could not raise enough volunteers and was disbanded in December 1940. Reformed in January, 1942, as No 10 (Interallied) Commando, it was made up of men from occupied territories.

No 10 Commando was organized as follows:

Headquarters British
No 1 Troop   French
No 2 Troop   Dutch
No 3 Troop   Miscellaneous (made up from Jews from occupied Hungary, Czechoslovakia, Greece and a strong contingent from Germany).

Belgian Commandos in Italy, 1944.

The Belgian Troop Headquarters

No 4 Troop	Belgian
No 5 Troop	Norwegian
No 6 Troop	Polish
No 7 Troop	Yugoslav
No 8 Troop	French
No 9 Troop	Belgian
No 10 Troop	Belgian

The shoulder title was No 10 COMMANDO, red on dark blue, in two sizes, large and small.

The French wore the same FRANCE shoulder title and cap badges as men in 4 Commando.

The Dutch wore No 10 COMMANDO shoulder title which they wore above their patch of the Lion of Orange over NEDERLAND, yellow on khaki. On the beret they wore the Lion of Orange in brass or BZ for officers.

The Belgian troops wore a large lettered shoulder title BELGIUM, red on dark blue; also red on khaki below No 10 COMMANDO shoulder title. On their beret they wore a rampant lion on a black backing.

The Norwegian troops wore the title NORGE, white on khaki, and a small Norwegian national flag in blue, red and white on khaki patch below the title No 10 COMMANDO. On the beret they wore 7 superimposed on H within a crowned wreath.

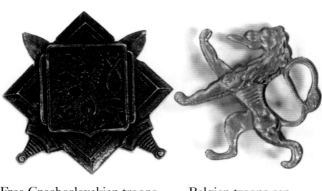

Free Czechoslovakian troops cap badge.

Belgian troops cap badge.

Free Czechoslovakian, pocket badge.

The Polish troops wore the title POLAND in large letters, red on dark blue above the No 10 COMMANDO title. On the beret they wore a metal badge of the Polish national eagle. No 7 and 3 Troops were made up of men from Yugoslavia, Hungary, Czechoslovakia, Germany and some of the men wore titles, i.e. CZECHOSLOVAKIA, red on dark blue. Some wore their own beret badges. SOE used these troops on secret missions.

No 11 Commando
Formed in 1940 from men of the Scottish Commando, it then became B Company, 2nd Special Service Battalion on the disbandment of the Special Service Brigade. In 1941 it became 11 Commando and later became C Troop, Layforce. It is not known why the shoulder title No 11 COMMANDO, red on dark blue, was made in early 1943 but never worn.

On the Balmoral or Tam-o-shanter a black hackle was worn.

No 12 Commando
This was formed in Northern Ireland in August 1940 from Irish and Welsh regiments. The first shoulder title was TWELVE, yellow letters on blue. Then it changed in 1942 to TWELVE COMMANDO, yellow on black, and again in late 1942 to No 12 COMMANDO yellow on green, either printed or woven. This last change, in early 1943 was to No 12 COMMANDO, red on dark blue, woven or printed.

No 14 Commando
This was formed in late 1942 for operations in the Arctic Circle against German bases supporting their troops on the Finnish Border and Luftwaffe bases bombing Russian Convoys. It was disbanded in late 1943. The only shoulder title was COMMANDO white on black.

Commando Signals
Formed from Special Service Brigade Signals in 1942 and served with Commando Headquarters. There were two Signalmen per Commando troop. This title was not in use long because men preferred to wear the normal Commando title. The shoulder title was COMMANDO SIGNALS, white on black, and then, in late 1942, red on black.

Commando Depot
This was formed in early 1942 when all Commando training was centralized at Achnacarry, in Scotland. It became the Commando Basic Training Centre by the end of 1942. They wore two shoulder titles. The first was COMMANDO over D. COMMANDO was woven in light blue and the D was in red on black. The second title was COMMANDO then D red on black.

Medical Commando

1st Medical Commando was formed on 26 June, 1945, from 1 Light Field AMG and was named 1 Medical Commando RAMC (light). This unit never saw active service and was disbanded in October, 1945. The shoulder title was 1 MEDICAL COMMANDO, red on dark blue.

2nd Medical Commando was formed from the remains of 1st Medical Commando but was never employed in active operations, and was disbanded in late 1945. The shoulder title was 2 MEDICAL COMMANDO light blue on black.

'On June 26th, 1945, orders were issued for the conversion of 1 LT FD AMG recently returned to the UK from Italy, into 1 Medical Commando RAMC (Light) with the effect from July 1st. On August 9th the unit was warned for service overseas in a tropical climate. It did not sail and in October was disbanded. 2 Medical Commando was formed out of its remains. This unit was not employed in active operations and with the ending of the war was disbanded in its turn.'

The Army Medical Services

Special Service Squadrons
In June, 1941, three tank squadrons were formed to support amphibious landings. These were entitled A, B and C Squadrons and wore a black shoulder title with Special "A", "B" and "C" Service (as appropriate) in white. Only B Squadron went into action – in the Madagascar landings of May, 1942. A Squadron was disbanded in the middle of that year and in July, B and C Squadrons formed the 1st Airborne Light Tank Squadron.

The Middle East Commandos 50, 51 and 52
50 Middle East Commando was formed in July, 1940, from men already serving out there. 51 Middle East Commando was formed in October of the same year from Jewish and Palestinian soldiers of the Auxiliary Military Pioneer Corps. Early in 1941, these two units amalgamated to become D Battalion of LAYFORCE and were otherwise known as the Combined (Middle East) Commando. 52 Middle East Commando was formed in November, 1940, and was sent to Crete where it suffered heavy casualties. On its return from there in the following summer it was disbanded.

Men of 50 Commando. Note the knuckle-duster knife badge.

Insignia

The unique feature of 50 Commando was their special knuckle-duster knife which they carried instead of the normal FS pattern knife. The cap badge was a small version of the knuckle-duster knife and, according to veterans, it was issued for the Crete operation. This comes in two sizes – the large flat type worn on the bush hat and the small type which was worn on side cap and field service cap. It was also common practice for men in the Middle East Commando to wear their own regimental cap badge and in some cases wear the knuckle-duster badge above it. They also wore a shoulder title M. E. COMMANDO, yellow on black. The Jewish and Palestine Arabs wore a metal shoulder title PALESTINE and a shoulder patch, a yellow Star of David on a purple, white, purple background.

No 62 Commando

Formed in mid-1941 under the command of Lieutenant David Stirling of the Scots Guards. For a short period the unit was designated number 1 Small Scale Raiding Force but in February, 1943, became the Special Air Service.
Insignia: none known.

The Royal Canadian Naval Beach Commando

This was formed in 1943 but did not see action until Normandy in 1944 and in South East Asia in 1945. The insignia worn was CANADA over COMMANDO red on blue. Melton head-dress was worn. This was a naval rating's cap with the cap tally H M C S; officers wore the RCN peaked cap.

The Royal Navy Commando

This was formed in 1941 for beach parties and changed its name to R N Commando in late 1941. In spring of 1942 the RN Beach Head Commando began to be formed. In order not to confuse them with the other Commando units, the RN Commandos were given letter designations using the phonetic alphabet of the time. Each unit was made up of two officers and twenty-two men. One officer was the Beach Master who wore a title BEACHMASTER instead of RN Commando. By 1943 there were twenty-two RN

Commando units which served in every theatre of war. The first shoulder title was ROYAL NAVY, white on black, and in the spring of 1942 was changed to R.N. COMMANDO white on black in woven and printed examples.

No 30 Commando
This unit was formed on 30 September, 1942, under the code name Special Engineering Unit and became 30th Assault Unit in 1943. It comprised three troops,

33 Troop (Royal Marine), 34 Troop (Army Commando), 36 Troop (Royal Navy or technical). The unit's job was to collect information, i.e. paperwork, maps, etc from enemy headquarters. This unit wore no shoulder title but wore a shoulder patch, a red 30 on a khaki background.

The Royal Marine Commandos

The Royal Marine Commandos were formed in 1943 from men of the RM Division. The commando were formed as follows:

40 (RM) Commando
Raised in February, 1942, as RM A Commando it became 40 (RM) Commando later that year. It absorbed 43 RM Commando in 1945, and disbanded in 1946. The shoulder title was 40 over ROYAL MARINE over COMMANDO, red on black, woven or printed.

41 (RM) Commando
Raised in October, 1942, as RM B Commando from 8th Battalion RM Division and 41 RM Commando in late October, 1942. Disbanded by 1946. The Shoulder title was 41 over ROYAL MARINE over COMMANDO, red on black, woven or printed.

42 (RM) Commando
Formed in 1943 from 1st Battalion RM Division. Served in Burma in 1944-45. The shoulder title was 42 over ROYAL MARINES over COMMANDO, red on black, woven or printed.

43 (RM) Commando
Formed from 2nd Battalion RM Division in mid 1943. The shoulder title was 43 over ROYAL MARINES over COMMANDO, red on black, woven or printed.

44 (RM) Commando
Formed from 3rd Battalion RM Division in mid-1943. Served in the Far East. There are two shoulder titles. The official title was 44 over ROYAL MARINE over COMMANDO, red on black, woven or printed. An unofficial title was No 44 COMMANDO, red on black. This was locally made. Woven examples only.

45 (RM) Commando
Formed from 5th Battalion RM Division in mid-1943. The shoulder title was No. 45 over ROYAL MARINES over COMMANDO red on black.

46 (RM) Commando
Formed from 9th Battalion RM Division in mid 1943. The shoulder title was 46 over ROYAL MARINES over COMMANDO, red on black, printed or woven.

A group of A Troop, 45 Royal Marine Commando, at Southampton before setting off for France. Seated right is Lance Corporal Henry Harden, RAMC, who would win a Victoria Cross in Holland, January 1945, and lose his life.

47 (RM) Commando
Formed from 10th Battalion RM Division mid-1943. The shoulder title was 47 over ROYAL MARINES over COMMANDO, red on black. Printed or woven.

48 (RM) Commando
Formed from 7th Battalion RM Division early in 1944. The shoulder title was 48 over ROYAL MARINES over COMMANDO, red on black, printed or woven.

By the end of the war Cash nametape examples were being used. All shoulder titles were worn in 1, 2 or 3-part constructions.

RM Commandos who were para-trained, wore a wing like the Army but the wings and canopy were red on a black backing. For a short period some men wore a straight Airborne title, red on black.

The Special Boat Sections (Army Commando)

In late 1940 or early 1941 the Army Commando formed two Special Boat Sections. No 1 Special Boat Section was formed as Folboat Section No 8 Commando, in November, 1940. Sent to the Middle East in March 1941, it was renamed Middle

East Folboat Section, then in 1942 became D Squadron Special Air Service and eventually became the nucleus of the Special Boat Squadron in late 1942. No 2 Special Boat Squadron which was formed in April 1942 was part of the 1st Special Service Brigade and was amalgamated with the Combined Operations Pilotage Parties under the command of Lieutenant Commander Clogstoun-Willmott, for training and other duties.

Insignia

The beret badge, which came in two variations, one in metal, the other in cloth, was a shield within a shield with a hand brandishing Excalibur and rising out of the water, with the letters SS at either side and a B below the waterline. The shoulder title was

Worn in 1944/45 Headquarters only.

red lettering on black which read COMMANDO S.B.S. and was worn with the Combined Operations badge as shown at the bottom of this page.

Combined Operations

Insignia

Designed by Lieutenant D. A. Grant RNVR in 1942, the badge, as described by Lord Mountbatten, consisted of a Tommy gun, an eagle and a stockless anchor, representing the Army, the Royal Air Force and the Royal Navy. The first badge was designed so that the manufacturers would be able to produce the required number of badges within a reasonable time; the embroidered badge came later. At this time it was made in three colours – red on dark blue, blue on white (Royal Navy only), and yellow on light blue, which was for US personnel. This badge was changed slightly; instead of an eagle it had an American eagle. The US Amphibious Forces badge was exactly the same as the new American eagle badge but on a red background. There is also a gold bullion on black variation for No 1 dress.

Chapter 2

The Special Air Service

The inspired creation of the young Lieutenant David Stirling, Scots Guards, the Special Air Service (SAS) came into being in August, 1941, first under the cover name of 62 Commando and then as L Detachment, the Special Air Service Brigade (an equally fictitious title). Although known to all as the SAS, it remained as L Detachment until January, 1943 when the 1st Special Air Service Regiment was formally established. In April, 1943, it was followed by the 2nd Regiment under David Stirling's brother Bill.

L Detachment consisted at first of two squadrons who were later joined by the Special Boat Squadron and later still, in 1942, by a French squadron raised under Stirling's direction and the Greek Sacred Squadron. (It is the tradition of the Greeks to raise a *Heros Lukos* unit when Greece is in peril. Previous two occasions were 379 BC and 1821.)

After a disastrous first raid, the SAS began to work hand in glove with the Long Range Desert Group, who generously supplied them with the means of mobility until they acquired their own armed jeeps in the middle of 1942.

A mixture of men from three Special Forces units exchange notes in North Africa – Long Range Desert Group, Special Air Service and Raiding Support Regiment. The SAS are wearing their sand-coloured berets.

This side cap belonged to Paddy O'Dowd, 1942.

Between January and April 1943 the Special Air Service were engaged in a number of missions to harass the enemy and reconnoitre their positions. These were carried out to coincide with the advance of the Eighth Army. During one of these operations, David Stirling, now a Lieutenant Colonel, was captured. The 1st SAS Regiment was then divided into the Special Raiding Squadron under Major Paddy Mayne, and the Special Boat Squadron under Major the Lord Jellicoe. These two forces were placed under the command of Raiding Forces, Middle East Forces, under Brigadier Turnbull.

In May 1943 Second Battalion Special Air Service Regiment was formed from a detachment of No 62 Commando and was commanded by Lieutenant Colonel Bill Stirling, brother of David Stirling, the founder of L Detachment.

In early 1944 the formation of HQ SAS Troop was established at Sorn Castle, Ayrshire. Under its command were 1st and 2nd SAS, with the newly created 3rd and 4th SAS which had been formed from French Parachutists, a Belgian SAS company and F Squadron Phantom Regiment.

Headgear

The earliest known piece of headgear was the white beret, but this is extremely rare. When it was first issued, the Australian and New Zealand members did not like it because of leg-pulling from the other units, so it was changed for a short while to khaki forage caps and side caps. Within a year this was replaced by a beige beret which was worn in North Africa and Italy, but when the unit came back to the UK and came under the command of Airborne Forces, they were told to take off their beige berets and replace them with the red beret which all Airborne forces were wearing.

Cap Badges

The badge, according to several books written on the SAS, was designed by Bob Tait. This badge, which is nicknamed 'the winged dagger', was supposed to be a winged representation of King Arthur's Excalibur; the local tailors knew nothing about Excalibur, but they did know that all the men used to carry the Fairburn Sykes

First SAS headgear – a white beret – here seemingly being worn with some self-consciousness. It was extremely unpopular because of the leg-pulling it attracted from other soldiers. R. Miles, New Zealand

The more popular sand-coloured beret. R. Miles, New Zealand

An officer of the Greek Sacred Squadron with the distinctive badge (example inset) on the right breast pocket. The first such unit was raised in 379 BC to fight the Spartans. They were massacred to a man at Thebes. The second occasion was in 1821 to fight the Turks. Once again the regiment was slain to a man. The third inauguration was the Greek Sacred Squadron of the SAS, raised in 1942.

dagger, so represented this. The badge was embossed in red, white and Cambridge blue threads on an Oxford blue shield with the motto Who Dares Wins. The motto is reportedly the suggestion of David Stirling himself. The badges come in various sizes and widths. This is due to the different manufacturers they used at various

1942   1942

1943

1944

Paddy Mayne wearing the large cloth cap badge of the Special Air Service early 1942.

times. There is a cast brass and white metal version of the cap badge, which comes in three or four variations. Some have the motto on and some do not. When foreign troops served with the SAS, some wore their own country's cap badges and the Greek Sacred Squadron wore its own breast badge and its own cap badge, but wore the SAS wing. (See page 75.)

Qualification Wings

The distinctive dark blue and light blue SAS parachute wings were designed by Jock Lewes, who had rowed for Oxford. He incorporated light blue since another original

Made in Egypt in 1942.

member, Lieutenant Langton, had rowed for Cambridge. The wing shape is based on the ancient Egyptian hieroglyphic representation for the solar deity.

Shoulder Titles

There are five shoulder titles to this unit. The first title to appear is 1st S.A.S. Cambridge blue on maroon, woven. The next one is 2nd S.A.S., Cambridge blue on maroon, woven. For a short period in 1944 the French members who formed the third SAS wore a title 3rd S.A.S. Cambridge blue on maroon which was hand woven, and was only worn for a very short period of time. By the end of 1944, or early 1945 the numbers were discontinued and the title S.A.S. white on maroon or Cambridge blue on maroon, appeared. The last title to appear was Special Air Service, Cambridge blue on maroon. There is no evidence that the 4th and 5th SAS ever wore titles.

SAS on parade on the occasion of the award of gallantry medals to its members – all are wearing the maroon beret of the Airbourne.

A mixture of maroon and sand–coloured berets at this parade.

Second Squadron, Second Special Air Service, Colchester, October 1945.

CB.0152

Chief Inspectorate of Clothing.

Pattern No. 13123

Badges arm:-

Parachutists S.A.S. Regt.

Approved

Date 2 - 3 - 46   Authority A.D.C. Patterns

&

SO4147 (W5) M11170/9329 1/41 10M C&R703

Chapter 3

Other Raiding Forces in the Middle East

T he SAS was by no means alone in its raiding activities as reference to the LRDG has already shown. The work of all raiders in the theatre was coordinated by a small headquarters at General Headquarters in Cairo.

The Long Range Desert Group

This unit was formed by Major Ralph Bagnold from volunteers from the 2nd New Zealand Cavalry Division, 27th (Machine Gun) Battalion and the 7th Anti-Tank Regiment. Because of its success, GHQ Middle East decided in December 1940 to double its size by adding a Guards Patrol, a Yeomanry Patrol of volunteers from the 1st Cavalry Division in Palestine, and another Commonwealth Patrol from Rhodesian volunteers. What had been loosely titled the Long Range Patrol was now officially designated the Long Range Desert Group (LRDG). Formed into squadrons A, B, C, D, the LRDG became so successful in the Middle East that in 1943 they had a new task – the desert watchers became coastwatchers in the Aegean.

On the night of 23 October, 1943, twenty-three men of A (NZ) Squadron and twenty-six men of B Squadron attempted to capture the island of Levita but, as a result of bad intelligence, no one knew that the garrison had been reinforced. B Squadron was overwhelmed immediately and A (NZ) Squadron isolated, pounded by air and pinned down by machine-gun fire. For 24 hours they fought with no hope of winning. On the night of 24 October, nine survivors of A Squadron and all of B Squadron met the rescue launches. On hearing of this disaster, the New Zealand government asked why no one had told them about this operation and why its nationals had been committed to a new theatre of war. The decision to withdraw the New Zealanders from the Long Range Desert Group was taken so A (NZ) Squadron was disbanded on 31 December, 1943.

By April, 1944, the LRDG was reorganized and reinforced and was placed under the command of Land Forces Adriatic with the role of an airborne/seaborne raiding force in Italy and the Balkans. It was disbanded in May 1945.

Insignia

Cap Badge
The cap badge was designed by Gunner C. O. Grimsey who had been stung three times by a scorpion. Grimsey survived but the scorpion died. Using the dead

scorpion as a model, Grimsey designed the badge of a scorpion within a wheel and it became the official insignia of the LRDG. The badge comes in brass, in bronze and in gold which was reportedly made from the rings of dead Germans.

In recent years a badge has appeared which is reportedly the first cap badge of the New Zealand men of the newly formed Long Range Patrol. But after an extensive search of records and photographs, it would appear that the only badge worn is the standard New Zealand Infantry badge. There is no evidence that the other badge was ever worn or made in Egypt. In the opinion of some leading collectors it could be a 'sweetheart' or an Old Comrade badge. It is made of thin silver with a gilt wash scorpion with the letters LRP over LRDG with NZ at each end of a scroll and has a pin backing. An example has been included to see if any more information is forthcoming.

Three types of headgear sporting the LRDG cap badge.

Shoulder Title

The shoulder title is LRDG in red lettering on a black background. There is also a slip-on which has black lettering on khaki. For a short period a serif-letter brass title was also worn. Some of the titles turn up pink or white. This is simply proof of the power of the Libyan sun.

The Indian Long Range Squadron

This Squadron was the 9th Army's version of the Long Range Desert Group. It was formed on 25 December, 1941, from volunteers from 3 Indian Motor Brigade and had four patrols. The Squadron was to operate behind enemy lines in Persia, Iraq and Syria should the Nazis break through the Balkans. As this did not happen, two of the patrols were attached to the LRDG, and in October, 1942 the two remaining patrols joined them as part of the 8th Army.

When the desert war was over, there was no employment for the Squadron and they were sent to India where they remained unemployed until the middle of 1944. They were then dispatched to the Persian-Afghan-Russian border to prevent Russian incursions into that area. They returned to India in 1947 where they were disbanded.

Insignia

The Cap Badge

The badge is crossed lances with a tablet in the centre with LR on it. It comes in brass for other ranks and silver for officers.

Shoulder Title

The shoulder title worn by the Squadron comes in two forms; the first is a cloth slip-on with the initials ILRS embroidered in gold on a blue oblong.

The second is a hand-cut, blackened brass shoulder title I.L.R.S.

No 1 Demolition Squadron (Popski's Private Army)

This was one of the most extraordinary units which formed part of the British Army during the Second World War. Raised in March, 1942, by Popski (Vladimir Peniakoff) a Russian refugee who had spent some time at Cambridge University and served as an engineer with a French company in Egypt. He had acquired a commission on the General List and served with the Libyan Arab Force where he was ordered to form a Libyan Arab Commando to gather intelligence in the area of that vast feature east of Benghasi, the Jebel Akhdar. He had acquired his nickname from the LRDG, with whom his small force had trained. It stuck! After seven months, during which they rescued over eighty Allied soldiers from prisoner of war cages, Popski found, on returning to Cairo, that in his absence his unit had been officially disbanded. With the news of the Allied landings in Algeria, Popski again went to GHQ and offered to form another irregular unit, with the aim of sabotaging enemy installations and raiding enemy supply lines between the advancing Eighth Army and the First Army moving east from Algeria.

Popski wearing PPA shoulder title and cap badge. Note his artificial left hand (see page 18).

The new unit began to assemble in mid-1942 with the official title of No 1 Demolition Squadron, but was commonly known as Popski's Private Army. Popski's men fought well in North Africa. They destroyed over thirty planes, 115 vehicles, many of which were armoured, captured over 600 prisoners and destroyed nearly 500,000 gallons of petrol.

When the Axis Armies surrendered in North Africa in May 1943 Popski and his men moved to Italy where they carried on raiding and wrecking as they had in North Africa, and in May 1945 crossed into Austria at Tarvisio. They were disbanded on 14 September 1945.

Insignia

Cap Badge

The cap badge comes in silver and also in brass and represents an astrolabe, an instrument for taking the altitude of stars for navigational purposes.

The first badges were made in cast silver with a pin fastening, but Popski wanted better quality and detail. He went to a silversmith in Cairo, where the first badges were cut and engraved by hand in brass, but this took too long so the silversmiths cast them in silver and finished them by hand. When Popski landed in Italy in 1943 he transferred his custom to Roman silversmiths who produced the badge in silver, brass and white metal.

Shoulder Titles

The first titles bore the letters P.P.A. in red on a black background but changed to white P.P.A. on a black background when they were in Italy. Popski had some brass titles made there and these can be seen being worn in 1946 in photographs of the Victory Parade through London.

The Raiding Support Regiment

Formed in mid-1943 to support the recently formed Raiding Force, the Raiding Support Regiment was made up of men from the Special Boat Squadron, the LRDG and the Greek Sacred Squadron. By October 1943 the Regiment acquired the name Raiding Support Regiment with the job of supporting raiding forces and bringing heavy weapons for partisan groups in Greece, Yugoslav and Albania. Under the command of Lieutenant Colonel Sir Thomas Devitt Bt, of the Seaforth Highlanders, the Regiment went from strength to strength and by the end of 1943 consisted of five batteries comprising:

A. machine-gun battery of twelve Vickers and captured Spandau medium machine-guns.
B. mortar battery of heavy mortars.
C. light AA battery of eighteen Browning and fifty heavy machine guns.
D. anti-tank battery of four Italian 47/32mm anti-tank guns.
E. mountain battery of four US 75mm pack howitzers.

The Regiment saw action on the Yugoslav mainland helping Tito's partisans, while other detachments raided the Dalmatian Islands and the coast of Albania, the largest contingent being sent to Greece.

The Regiment was disbanded in early 1945.

Insignia

Cap Badge
Captain D. C. Rose, Royal Artillery, designed the cap badge, a winged mailed fist (representing armed help from the air grasping a bare hand, (coming to the aid of local partisan groups), raised from a castle turret (signifying beleaguered partisans in their mountain stronghold) which sat upon a scrolled motto.

Lieutenant Colonel Devitt picked the motto from Chapter 16, verse 13, of the first letter of St Paul to the Corinthians: 'Quit you like men be strong', which was shortened to 'Quit you like men'. Some have suggested that it was also intended to be read backwards and referred to the Germanic-looking eagle. The badge comes in two variations. The first is machine-stitched with the motto stitched on separately. These were made locally. The second is handmade. The badge was usually stitched on a perspex backing and was worn on either a black or a beige beret.

Wing
The regiment wore the same wing as the SAS on the right arm.

Shoulder Title
The title comes in two forms, the first being in metal and reads RSR. It was attached to a white slip-on. The second was RSR stitched on a slip-on. The letters were in black on a khaki base.

Made in Yugoslavia in 1944.

Member of the Raiding Support Regiment showing his SAS wing.

Land Forces Adriatic

This group was formed in 1944 from the Long Range Desert Group, 50, 51 and 52 Commandos, the East African Irregular Companies, Raiding Support Regiment, Special Boat Service, a US Operational Group, an Assyrian Parachute Company, plus unnamed secret forces. Their attacks were more relentless and formidable than those of earlier Raiding Forces, involving commandos and artillery, as well as other troops, and lasting for some months. However, even they must have been surprised when, in September and October 1944, one party ended up freeing half of Greece!

Insignia
The formation sign worn was a white Pegasus swimming on an oval blue or black patch; it comes in printed or woven variations.

The hundred or so men of the Yugoslav-speaking Americans of 3 Contingent US Operational Group wore a shoulder title which was yellow on black, and a yellow combined ops patch which was made locally.

Made in Cairo in 1943.

Chapter 4

Raiding Forces in the Far East

The Chindits

This group, the biggest of the special forces of the Second World War, was formed by Orde Wingate in India in 1942 from a motley collection of soldiers: from the Bush Warfare School, volunteers from eight British Commando units in Britain, a battalion of Burma Rifles, a Gurkha battalion, the 13th Battalion Kings Regiment which was itself made up of older men and rejects from other regiments. After six months of hard and punishing training the men were ready for action. They were officially called 77th Indian Brigade (The Chindits).

They got their name of Chindits as a corruption of the word 'chinthe' which is a lion-headed dragon, the guardian of the entrance to every pagoda in Burma.

The 77th Indian Brigade was so successful in its first mission behind the lines (from February–May, 1943) that it was decided to enlarge the force. The new force became known as Special Force or the 3rd Indian Infantry Division. It was made up of six brigades and other supporting units. Each brigade was split into columns which were numbered where possible in accordance with the old battalion system of pre-1881; for example, the York and Lancaster Regiment came from the 65th and 84th of Foot and its columns were numbered accordingly.

The Special Force was made up as follows:

3rd West African Brigade
HQ (*Brigadier A. H. Gillmore succeeded by Brigadier Abdy Ricketts*) (column 10)
6th Battalion Nigeria Regiment (columns 39 & 66)
7th Battalion Nigeria Regiment (columns 29 & 35)
12th Battalion Nigeria Regiment (columns 12 & 43)

14th British Infantry Brigade (ex 70 Division)
HQ (Brigadier Thomas Brodie) (column 59)
54th Field Company Royal Engineers (support)
1st Battalion Bedfordshire & Hertfordshire Regt. (columns 16 & 61)
7th Battalion Royal Leicestershire Regiment (columns 47 & 74)
2nd Battalion The Black Watch (columns 42 & 73)
2nd Battalion York & Lancaster Regiment (columns 65 & 84)

16th British Infantry Brigade (ex 70 Division)

HQ (*Brigadier Bernard Fergusson*)	(column 99)
51/69 Field Regiments Royal Artillery (as Infantry)	(columns 51 & 69)
2nd Field Company Royal Engineers	(support)
2nd Battalion The Queen's Royal Regiment	(columns 21 & 22)
2nd Battalion Royal Leicestershire Regiment	(columns 17 & 71)
45th Reconnaissance Regiment (as Infantry)	(columns 45 & 54)

23rd British Infantry Brigade (ex 70 Division)

HQ (*Brigadier Lance Perowne*)	(column 32)
60th Field Regiment Royal Artillery (as Infantry)	(columns 60 & 68)
12th Field Company Royal Engineers	(support)
2nd Battalion Duke of Wellingtons Regiment	(columns 33 & 76)
4th Battalion Border Regiment	(columns 34 & 55)
1st Battalion Essex Regiment	(columns 44 & 56)

77th Indian Infantry Brigade

HQ (*Brigadier Michael Calvert*)	(column 25)
Mixed Field Company Royal Engineers/Royal Indian Engineers	
1st Battalion King's Regiment (Liverpool)	(columns 81 & 82)
1st Battalion Lancashire Fusiliers	(columns 20 & 50)
1st Battalion South Staffordshire Regiment	(columns 38 & 80)
3rd Battalion 6th Gurkha Rifles	(columns 36 & 63)
3rd Battalion 9th Gurkha Rifles (to 111 Bde later)	(columns 57 & 93)
142 Company Hong Kong Volunteers	(support)

111th Indian Infantry Brigade

HQ (*Brigadier 'Joe' Lentaigne, succeeded first by Major Jack Masters and then Brigadier 'Jumbo' Morris*)	(column 48)
Mixed Field Company Royal Engineers/Royal Indian Engineers	(support)
2nd Battalion Kings Own Royal Regiment	(columns 41 & 46)
1st Battalion Cameronians	(columns 26 & 90)
3rd Battalion 4th Gurkha Rifles	(columns 30 & 40)
4th Battalion 9th Gurkha Rifles (Morris force)	(columns 49 & 94)

Other Units Included:

Bladet (Commando Engineers) *(Major Blain)*
Danforce (Kachin Levies) *(Lieutenant Colonel Herring)*
2nd Battalion Burma Rifles
Four troops 160th Field Regiment Royal Artillery (in the artillery role)
Four troops 69th Light Anti-Aircraft Regiment Royal Artillery (in the artillery role)

Shoulder slip-on made in India in 1944.

Locally made bush hat badge in 1944.

Column badges of the York
and Lancaster Regiment.

Logistic Units

The principal aim of General Wingate's second Chindit operation, Operation THURSDAY, was to harass the Japanese flow of reinforcements and supplies to the two Japanese divisions facing the American General Stilwells's Chinese forces in Northern Burma and to enable him to advance to the River Salween and make Northern Burma safe, so that the vital Ledo road into China could be constructed, thereby allowing the renewal of the flow of arms and warlike stores into China which had been stopped by the loss of the Burma road from Rangoon in 1942. Unlike the first Chindit operation (LONGCLOTH), there would be massive airlift available to fly in the whole force, except 16 Brigade (which would march) and all its logistic support and even vehicles. After twenty weeks of rigorous training, the force was ready and the operation was launched in the first week of March, 1944. Whilst substantial damage to the Japanese was achieved, the force paid a very heavy price

This is YOUR badge. It means that :—
You are a member of SPECIAL FORCE.
You are proud of SPECIAL FORCE.
All ranks SPECIAL FORCE are proud of you.

1. You have come out from the middle of BURMA, where you have done your job in a manner which has thrilled the whole world. You have hit the JAP where it hurts him most—in the guts.

You have shown determination and endurance. You have out-manœuvred and out-fought the enemy. You have every right to be proud of yourself.

Now you are tired, and need rest and bucking up. I am doing my best to see that you get the rest which is your due.

2. Your Chinthe badge will attract attention and comment. You must see that the reputation you and your pals have earned in battle does not suffer from your behaviour out of battle.

The badge of the FORCE should show that you are not only " SPECIAL " in fighting but also " SPECIAL " in discipline and behaviour.

This is a young show which has already made a name. See to it that you do nothing to let it down.

Whether in or out of barracks or on leave, your bearing, turn-out and behaviour should be that of a man belonging to a picked unit, which is what you are.

3. You will be asked questions by others about your job and experiences, but there are certain subjects about which you must NOT talk. If you do, you will endanger the lives of those still in BURMA and those who go in next time.

You must NOT tell anyone what units are part of SPECIAL FORCE.

You must NOT talk about the details of how you went in and out of BURMA, how you got your rations, how the air helped you, and how your wireless messages were sent and received.

You must NOT talk about your special training, equipment and arms.

The safety of your comrades in SPECIAL FORCE depends on your loyalty and good sense.

I know that I can depend on you to be discreet.

4. Finally you must remember that the fine work you have done is not the end of the war. We have won this round on points—in the next round we will go in for a knock out. You are now fully trained and know your stuff. Your job is to train the new fellows and lead them next time. Teach them to kill with every round. Teach them that the jungle is nothing like as bad as it is cracked up to be. Teach them that though it's a tough job it's a man's job, a job worth doing, and a job thats got to be done if we want to get back to Civvy Street quickly.

Good luck and I hope you have a good leave.

Maj-Gen.,
Comd. Special Force.

26th April 1944.

for success and would ultimately return to India in tatters, leaving many men in jungle graves, not only as battle casualties but also as the victims of disease.

Insignia

Badges
The shoulder patch consists of a yellow-headed dragon, with a small pagoda in yellow on a blue or black background. It comes in either yellow cotton or gold bullion. The shoulder title is slightly curved with the word CHINDIT on it, in white cotton or gold bullion with a rope border on either blue or black background. Because of the unusual nature of this special force, some of the columns wore their own badges either as headgear or as slip-on on their shoulder board. The 65th column wore a red square or diamond patch with a 65 in white in the centre; the 84th wore a black square with a yellow 84 in the centre; the 55th column wore a yellow 55 on a green oblong patch; the 142 Company Hong Kong Volunteers wore the shoulder title 142 in blue on a red background; the Duke of Wellington's Regiment wore a white DW on a black square. It is possible that other columns wore insignia but this information is not available. The men who were parachute-trained wore a parachute wing on a black background.

The Malayan Peoples Anti-Japanese Army

Formed in 1941 from the Malayan Communist Party, this unit was disbanded on 1 December, 1945. Around 200 Chinese were recruited and trained by the MCP. Although not under British control, the group had contact with British officers who had worked behind Japanese lines in Malaya. Contact between them and the British officers was lost between February, 1942, and May, 1943, but it played an important part in organizing the resistance movement which became known as the Malayan Peoples Anti-Japanese Army (MPAJA). Initially there was considerable offensive action against the Japanese, but as the latter tightened their control of the area, this came to an end and efforts had to be concentrated on maintaining their existence in the jungle. Those British servicemen who had remained at large were cared for and invited to help with training but had no say in the running of the army. British contact was re-established in August, 1943, by a party from India, made up of Chinese-speaking Canadians and members of SOE. It was later agreed that the MPAJA would accept orders from the Allied Forces. On the Allied side, the British undertook to arm, train and supply the MPAJA which by this time had developed into a very large organization, divided into eight groups, each with its own leader. Unfortunately, the British were unable to keep to their side of the bargain as all contact with India was lost until February, 1945, after which date British liaison was re-established. From then on the MPAJA was organized into five patrols of not less than 100 men each. British officers had operational command but internal command was carried out by the MPAJA's own officers. By the time of the Japanese surrender, there were over 4000 members of the MPAJA under the control of British liaison officers. It remained mobilized after the Japanese surrender.

Insignia

Cap Badge

The Cap Badge comes in three types of metal; the first is in cast brass. This was worn by the Europeans and local Malayans who were not members of the Communist Party. The badge design is a tiger with the scroll Malaya in English, Chinese and Malayan. In 1943 the British SOE recruited Chinese-speaking Canadians who, when they were trained and sent to Malaya, adopted the same cap badge, but in cast silver with either red or black highlights.

The third badge was worn by a group of Malayan levies raised in 1944. It was made of lead with a black highlighted centre.

The Malayan Communist Party members refused to wear the tiger cap badge but instead wore three red stars in a pyramid shape on a black background.

Shoulder Title

There is no evidence that they wore any shoulder title.

David Buxton, England.

Mission 204

This was formed from Mission 101 and LAYFORCE which had been fighting the Italians in Abyssinia in June, 1941. Its aim was to give help to the Chinese General Chiang Kai-shek in fighting the Japanese. The Chinese border with Burma also gave them an important role in supplying the resistance there, should the Japanese decide to invade Burma. Their task was to raise five battalions of Chinese guerrillas who would become the focus of resistance to the Japanese. The mission personnel were to act as advisors to the Chinese.

However, during the training of this force, the Japanese attacked Pearl Harbour in December, 1941, with the result that two contingents were detached from Mission 204 and redesignated Special Service Detachments (SSD). They were placed under the command of the Burma Army as the defence of Burma had become paramount.

SSD 1 and 2 were placed under General Orde Wingate's command and in April SSD 2 destroyed the bridge carrying the Kengtung–Meiktila road while SSD 1 were kept busy around Kengtung with Chinese troops. SSD 1 was attacked and the second-in-command, Jocelyn Nicholls, was killed. The troop was in danger of being cut off, so it was decided to make for Lashio, but then news arrived that the Japanese had captured it, and they were obliged to make for Kunming in China. It took them six weeks to get there, delayed by the terrain, sickness and arguments between Yunnanese troops and Chiang Kai-shek's army. In July SSD 1 were flown back to India. There they learnt that SSD 2 had attempted to get back to India but the dense jungle had forced them to split into small groups, many of whom were never seen again. Some made it back to India, while others joined Stilwell's men in Burma. The Mission was disbanded in August 1942.

Mission 204 Special Service Detachment No 1 at Taunngyi, Southern Shan Stat Burma 3 February 1942 wearing the distinctive fighting dagger cap badge.

Insignia

Mission 204, for some reason, wore a silver badge similar to the men of 50 Commando. This may be because some of the men from the Middle East Commando actually formed Mission 204.

V FORCE

This was formed in 1942 in the Assam and Bengal regions of India to act as Fifth Columnists should the Japanese enter that area from Burma. It was known as Force V at first but later became V Force. Its main job was to provide jungle intelligence for an area ten miles in front of the 14th Army's forward troops. As the 14th Army captured more and more of Burma, the need for V Force lessened and by June, 1945, it was decided that only those with parachute training, A Group, were needed to chase the Japanese over the border into China.

Insignia

The Cap Badge
The cap badge was a pair of crossed fighting knives with a V superimposed on it, resting on a scroll with the words FORCE in the centre. It comes in blackened brass and in silver variations. This was worn on the beret or cap; on the bush hat they wore V. FORCE in red on a black oblong patch.

Shoulder Title
The shoulder title comes with the words V. FORCE and is in red on a black curved background.

D FORCE

This was a deception unit. It was formed in 1941 in Iraq with the name Force X; in 1942 it became 303 Indian Armoured Brigade. In 1943 it was ordered to India where its new title was 303 Indian Brigade. There it was employed in three areas; 51 Observation Squadron was at Imphal, 52, 54 and 55 Squadrons were on the Arakan front, while 53 and 56 Squadrons were with the Chindits in northern Burma. Their job was to organize phoney attacks and thus draw the enemy's fire. They proved something of a nuisance to the enemy but their successes were not as great as originally hoped, mainly due to the damage that the tropical climate did to their fire-crackers. They returned to base in 1944 where they were amalgamated with 4 and 5 Light Scout Car Companies and the squadrons became companies with the following numbers and make-up:

> 51 – Punjabi Mussulman; 52 – Pathan; 53 – Jat; 54 – British; 55 – Sikh
> 56 – British; 57 – Punjabi Mussulman; 58 – British

This new unit was renamed D Force in October, 1944, and by the beginning of 1945, all except 56 Company were in action in Burma. Operations this time were much more successful; one member of 58 Company, Lieutenant Claud Raymond, won the Victoria Cross (posthumously) for providing a successful diversion and thus causing the enemy to flee. D Force returned to India in mid 1945 and 54, 56 and 58 Companies were amalgamated to form 59 and 60 Companies. After this time, however, their expertise was no longer required and the Force was disbanded in 1946.

Insignia
D Force wore a shoulder patch D. FORCE, red on dark green. This was also worn on the bush hat.

THE LUSHAI BRIGADE

This force was formed in March, 1944, to protect India from the Japanese if they decided to invade via the Lushai Hills. The Japanese had originally started their attack through Imphal and it was felt that, when they realized there were easier routes into India, they would change direction through these hills which were poorly defended.

It was formed at short notice from a combination of guerrilla and regular army troops under the command of Brigadier Marindin who, for the previous three months, had been in charge of V Force. The men making up this force came from:

1/9 Jats; 1 Bihar Regiment; 5 and 35 Indian Anti-Tank
Companies; 7/14 Punjab Regiment; 1616 Porter Corps
Company; 77 Field Ambulance, plus; 1 Assam Rifles,
5 and 8 V Ops Units; Lushai Scouts; Western Chin Levies.

Despite the monsoon, this force had been so successful by June that it was decided
to widen its efforts into full-scale operations in order to drive out the Japanese. By
the end of September the Brigade had caused the enemy serious losses of both men
and equipment and by January, 1945, had forced them out of Gangaw. Although it
was not realized at the time, this was to be their last action.

Insignia

Badge
The unit badge was a formation sign – a white V with
a head of a mython, the wild cattle indigenous to the
Lushai Hills in white in the centre of the V, with black
edgings on a red background.

Shoulder Title
The unit did not wear a special shoulder title but some
men who had come from V Force wore the V Force
shoulder title (see V Force for description).

Chapter 5

Airborne Forces

The Parachute Regiment

The Regiment was formed from No 2 Commando which in June, 1940, had been transferred to parachute duties. By November 1940 it was decided to change the name to 11 Special Air Service Battalion with a headquarters, a parachute wing and a glider wing.

By August, 1941, the parachute wing was reorganized into a battalion headquarters and four companies; then in September 1941 it was officially given the title 1st Parachute Battalion. By November 1941 it was decided to raise a second parachute battalion, then a third, and subsequently, by January, 1942, a fourth. The four battalions were then put into the 1st Parachute Brigade. When it was decided to form a 2nd Parachute Brigade, the 4th Battalion moved to the 2nd Brigade and the 5th Parachute Battalion was formed from the 7th Battalion the Cameron Highlanders in May, 1942, with the designation 5th (Scottish) Parachute Battalion.

The 6th Battalion was formed from the 10th Battalion Royal Welch Fusiliers in August, with the designation 6th (Royal Welch) Parachute Battalion, to complete the Brigade. The 7th (Light Infantry) Parachute Battalion was formed from the 10th Battalion Somerset Light Infantry in November 1942.

The 8th (Midland) Parachute Battalion was formed from the 13th Battalion Royal Warwickshire Regiment in the same month.

The 9th (Eastern and Home Counties) Parachute Battalion was formed from the 10th Battalion Essex Regiment in December, 1942.

The 10th Parachute Battalion was formed from volunteers from the 2nd Battalion Royal Sussex Regiment and units under Middle East command in March, 1943.

The 11th Parachute Battalion was formed from volunteers from units under Middle East command.

The 12th (Yorkshire) Parachute Battalion was formed from the 10th (East Riding) Battalion the Yorkshire Regiment (Green Howards) in May, 1943.

The 13th (Lancashire) Parachute Battalion was formed from 2nd /4th Battalion South Lancashire Regiment in July 1943.

The 14th Parachute Battalion was formed from the 4th Battalion Royal Hampshire Regiment in May 1947.

The 15th Parachute Battalion was formed from the 1st Battalion King's Liverpool Regiment in India in 1945.

The 16th Parachute Battalion was formed from the 1st Battalion South Staffordshire Regiment in India in 1945.

SPECIAL ARMY ORDER

THE WAR OFFICE,

31st *August*, 1942

20/GENERAL/6006   A.O. 128/1942

Formation of Glider Pilot Regiment and Parachute Regiment

The following regiments have been formed as Units of the Army Air Corps, the formation of which was notified in Army Order 21 of 1942 :—

Glider Pilot Regiment with effect from 24th February, 1942.

Parachute Regiment with effect from 1st August, 1942.

By Command of the Army Council,

The 17th Parachute Battalion was formed from volunteers from the North East of England in Augst 1945.

The 18th Parachute Battalion was formed from civilian volunteers from the Birmingham area in May, 1947.

The 21st Independent Company, the Parachute Regiment (1st Airborne Division) was formed from volunteers from existing parachute units in June, 1942.

The 22nd Independent Company, the Parachute Regiment (6th Airborne Division) was formed from volunteers from existing parachute units in May, 1943.

Insignia

Cap Badge

The cap badge was the same as the Army Air Corps (see page 112) until May, 1943 when a new badge was authorized. This consisted of a pair of wings outspread horizontally; in the centre was an opened parachute with the royal crest on top. It came in silver or bronze for officers and white metal for other ranks and, in 1943, a chocolate brown, or silver grey plastic economy badge was made.

Collar Badges
At first they wore the collar badges of the Army Air Corps, but in May 1943 when they got their new cap badge, the new collars were a small version of the cap badge and came in the same metals, but not in plastic.

Shoulder Titles and Patches
The first shoulder titles with the word PARACHUTE in light blue on maroon appeared in early August, 1941, while they were still serving with the 11th Special Air Service Battalion. Previous to this Paratroopers and Glider pilots wore a printed curved airborne title in light blue on maroon; in 1941 the Pegasus patch appeared; the badge was of Bellerophon astride Pegasus, in pale blue on dark maroon. This was to be worn by all airborne forces and in facing pairs. Then in September, 1941, on the formation of the 1st Battalion, the title changed to a curved title with the word PARACHUTE, with a 1 for 1st Parachute Battalion, 2 for the 2nd Battalion, 3 for the 3rd Battalion and 4 for the 4th Battalion; this is the rarest of all the titles. These titles were unofficial and later it was decided to remove the numbers to hide the identity of the battalions. These titles were worn until August, 1942, when the Parachute Regiment was

officially formed. The title was then changed to PARACHUTE REGIMENT, dark blue on light blue and comes in printed or woven examples. At this time the title PARATROOP REGIMENT, dark blue on light blue appeared but was never worn. As well as the new title they were also to wear the Pegasus patch, light blue on maroon; the title AIRBORNE again comes in light blue on maroon.

The 5th Parachute Battalion wore the shoulder title AIRBORNE until they received the regimental title. They also wore the Balmoral bonnet with the Hunting Stuart tartan backing with the Army Air Corps badge on it. This was worn until 1944 when they received the red beret and regimental cap badge, but still wore the Hunting Stuart tartan backing.

The 6th Parachute Battalion wore no special title but was granted permission to wear the Royal Welch Fusiliers black ribbon flash attached to the back of the collar.

The 7th Parachute Battalion wore a light infantry green epaulette tab on the battle-dress.

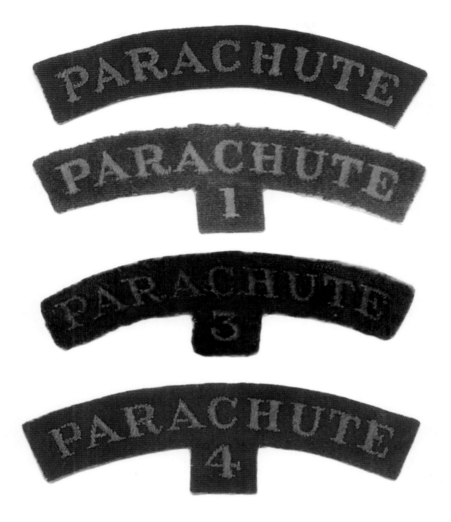

The 8th Parachute Battalion wore a dark blue epaulette tab on the battle-dress.

The 9th Parachute Battalion wore a maroon epaulette tab on the battle-dress.

The 10th Parachute Battalion wore a light blue, yellow and dark blue epaulette.

The 12th Yorkshire Parachute Battalion wore the epaulette tab YORKSHIRE in black on light blue.

The 13th Parachute Battalion wore a black epaulette tab on the battle-dress.

The 21st Independent Parachute Company wore a title PARACHUTE with XXI below light blue on maroon.

The 22nd Independent Parachute Company wore a light blue and white epaulette tab on the denison smock only. It is also claimed that they wore the title XX11 in light blue on maroon, but there is no written or photographic evidence to confirm this.

There are two more titles that appear and these were worn sometime in North Africa. Both fit on the epaulette; the first is PR in black on a khaki slip-on, the other is a metal shoulder title PARA.

Parachute Qualification Wing
The Parachute Qualification Wing was introduced in March 1941 for all ranks who had passed through the Parachute Training School. The wing comes in a variety of shapes, sizes and colours. At first the wing was issued in all white, i.e. white parachute and wing. This was shortlived and was changed to a light blue wing with a white parachute on a khaki background. These were issued at first in an oblong shape, then later the men used to cut them down to a half-moon shape and later still, it was cut to the shape of the wing.

The wing was worn on the right arm below the shoulder title and above the Pegasus patch. There is also photographic evidence that the wing was worn on the parachute helmet on the left-hand side; the reason for this is not known.

To non-regular parachute troops or instructors, a different badge was issued; this was a white parachute on a khaki square and comes in woven or screen-printed on cotton. It was commonly known as the Light-Bulb. It comes in two patterns; the first was a white parachute with a figure of a man on the end of the canopy ropes; this was screen-printed on green cotton. The second pattern as described above.

Parachute Instructors Qualification Badge
The badge was a parachute within a laurel wreath, light blue on dark blue. It is also known that instructors in India wore a white parachute with black laurel leaves on

Early photograph
of men of the
newly formed
Parachute unit,
May, 1941.

National flag worn by British troops during assaults on enemy-held territory (D-Day, Rhine Crossing, Greece).

a grey background. One oddity was a wing made out of Perspex. It was made in a POW camp sometime in 1944.

Some RAF personnel wore a wing which had a white canopy with light blue wings on an RAF blue backing.

The Glider Pilot Regiment

This was originally formed as the Glider wing of 11 Special Air Service Battalion and in December, 1941, became the first Glider Regiment. On 21 December 1941 it was decided to form the Army Air Corps and within it the Glider Pilot Regiment was to be formed; thus, on 27 February 1942 the First Glider Pilot Regiment was formed and in August 1942 the Second Glider Pilot was formed.

Insignia

Cap Badge
Same as the Army Air Corps.

Shoulder Title
On the formation of the regiment the title said GLIDER PILOT REGT. It was dark blue on light blue, with a 1 beneath for the 1st Battalion and a 2 in exactly the same colours for the 2nd Battalion. By early 1943 they had got rid of the numbers and just wore the title GLIDER PILOT REGT.

When the regiment was serving in the Middle East, a metal shoulder title, which fitted on the epaulette, appeared, which said Glider P in brass.

Qualification Wing
The wing was introduced in late 1942 for staff sergeants, first class pilots, and officer pilots. The wing was a large light blue wing on either side of the royal crest, on a black background, and came in two sizes, large and small. There are variations known on a khaki background and in bullion.

The second pilot wing was introduced in 1944. This was a gold G

GLIDER PILOT REGT.
1

GLIDER PILOT REGT.
2

GLIDER PILOT REGT.

GLIDER PILOT REGT.

GLIDER PILOT REGT.

GLIDER P.

within a gold circle with light blue wings on either side, on a black background. Both of these were worn over the left breast pocket.

Oddity
When the regiment was the Glider Wing of the 11th Special Air Service Battalion, some men wore an RAF-type wing with a small V, with short lines emanating from either side within a circle. The wing was on either side of the circle. It was all white on a black background.

The Army Air Corps

The Corps was formed on 21 December, 1941, as an administrative unit with the task of controlling the everyday administrative tasks of the Glider Pilot Regiment and, on 1 August, 1942, the Parachute Regiment, and finally in January 1944, the Special Air Service.

Insignia

Cap Badge
The cap badge was introduced in August 1942 and consisted of an eagle with outspread wings, head facing left, on a laurel wreath topped with a king's crown,

Made in North Africa in cast brass 1942/1943.

SPECIAL ARMY ORDER

THE WAR OFFICE,
27th February, 1942

ROYAL WARRANT

Formation of the Army Air Corps

GEORGE R.I.

20 / General / 6006

WHEREAS WE deem it expedient to authorize the formation of a corps to be entitled the Army Air Corps;

A.O. 21 / 1942

S.R.O. 325 / 1942

OUR WILL AND PLEASURE IS that the Army Air Corps shall be deemed to be a corps for the purposes of the Army Act, the Reserve Forces Act, 1882, and the Territorial and Reserve Forces Act, 1907;

OUR FURTHER WILL AND PLEASURE IS that the Schedule attached to the Warrant of His late Majesty King George V dated 27th February, 1926,* shall be amended as shown in Part I of the Schedule attached to this Our Warrant;

LASTLY, OUR WILL AND PLEASURE IS that the rates of pay of personnel of Our Army Air Corps shall be as prescribed in Part II of the Schedule attached to this Our Warrant.

Given at Our Court at St. James's, this 24th day of February, 1942, in the 6th year of Our Reign.

By His Majesty's Command,

P. J. GRIGG.

* Army Order 49 of 1926.

with a semi-circular bar which read A.A.C. It was in silver or bronze for officers and white metal for other ranks. In 1943 a chocolate brown or silver grey plastic economy badge was made.

Collar badge
This was a smaller version of the cap badge in silver or bronze for officers and white metal for other ranks.

Shoulder title
The shoulder title read ARMY AIR CORPS; it was dark blue on light blue. This title was worn at the end of 1942 by men of HQ. In 1943 an epaulette tab with AAC in black on khaki was worn.

The Airborne Corps Units

No 1 Air Troop Royal Engineers was formed in September 1941 and converted to
  1st Parachute Squadron RE in June 1942.
2nd Parachute Squadron RE was formed in October 1942.
3rd Parachute Squadron RE was formed in November 1942.
16th Parachute Field Ambulance was formed in April 1942.
225th. Parachute Field Ambulance was formed in July 1943.
250th Light Para Company RASC.
93rd (Airborne) Company RASC.
63rd (ABN) Coy RASC.
253rd ABN Re-supply CCA./Lug Bde.
Nos 749 & 799 Air Despatch Companies RASC were formed early in 1944.
Royal Army Ordnance Corps.
Royal Engineers.

Insignia
The air despatch companies of the RASC wore the shoulder title AIRBORNE woven
in yellow on dark blue instead of the title RASC yellow on dark blue, and below the

shoulder title they wore a square patch with a yellow Dakota aircraft on royal blue; it was woven or printed and worn on both arms. Beneath this patch they wore the title AIR DESPATCH, in yellow on blue.

The Air Troop Royal Engineers' first title was a small curved AIRBORNE in light blue on maroon. This was changed to ROYAL ENGINEERS PARACHUTE in red on black when the squadron converted. Then, in 1943, it changed again to read Royal Engineers, in blue on red.

The 2nd and 3rd Parachute Squadrons wore just the ROYAL ENGINEERS in blue on red.

The 16th Parachute Field Ambulance wore RAMC.

The 225th Parachute Field Ambulance for a very short time wore the shoulder title AMBULANCE in light blue on maroon.

The Royal Army Ordnance Corps wore for a short period the title ORDNANCE FIELD PARK in yellow on dark blue. Then, they went back to wearing RAOC, in blue on a scarlet background.

Officers of the REME preparing a jeep for an air drop, 1944.

1st AIR-LANDING BRIGADE

In October, 1941, the 31st Independent Brigade was chosen for the role as the 1st Air-Landing Brigade. The brigade was made up as follows:

Brigade Headquarters and Signal Section
1st Battalion Border Regiment
2nd Battalion South Staffordshire Regiment
2nd Battalion Oxfordshire and Buckinghamshire Light Infantry
1st Battalion Ulster Rifles
31st Independent Reconnaissance Company
223rd Anti-Tank Company RA
9th Field Company RE
181st Field Ambulance RAMC
31st Infantry Brigade Ordnance Workshop Field Park RAOC
31st Independent Infantry Brigade Company RASC
31st Independent Infantry Brigade Provost Section
1 Company Troop-Carrying Vehicles RASC

Insignia
For a short period the 31st Independent Brigade wore a shoulder patch which was a heraldic bull rising from a crown in red on a black background, in facing pairs.

Second Lieutenant T. Stafford and Lieutenant Williamson 1941. Border Museum

The early versions of this badge were painted. When the Brigade was converted to Air-Landing Brigade, a printed variation appeared, but somewhat smaller in size. By early 1942 this had disappeared and was replaced by the Pegasus patch and straight AIRBORNE title.

1st Airborne Division Provost Company wore the title PROVOST in black on red.

181st Field Ambulance wore the title Royal Army Medical Corps in gold on maroon with serifs.

1st Battalion Border Regiment on becoming glider-borne troops were still wearing the shoulder title BORDER white on red or the slip-on black on khaki. This was changed unofficially at first to read BORDER in yellow on a green background with a yellow or green stitching onto purple background.

The unit also had company epaulette colours yellow for Headquarters, green A Coy, white B Coy (but then this changed to purple, to avoid being confused with the officer cadet shoulder strip designation), red C Coy, pale blue D Coy, dark blue S Coy and black T, later R, Coy.

Qualification Badges (worn by all units of the Brigade)

Glider badge: Horsa glider woven in blue cotton on a khaki oval granted as a glider qualification badge after three flights and was worn in most cases by members of the battalion on the lower right sleeve on the battle-dress blouse. Also see parachute qualification badge (light bulb) above. The men who qualified for that badge wore it on the lower right sleeve above the glider badge.

2nd Battalion South Staffordshire Regiment

The Battalion wore the shoulder title SOUTH STAFFORD white on red; on becoming Glider borne troops they wore the title S. STAFFORDS yellow on maroon.

2nd Battalion Oxfordshire & Buckinghamshire Light Infantry

Between 1941 and early 1943 they wore the title FIFTY-SECOND in red with yellow edges on blue. Then in the spring of 1943 the Battalion was ordered to wear the regimental title OXF. & BUCKS, white on red; some members on their walking out dress wore OXFORD & BUCKS LI yellow on dark green.

1st Battalion Royal Ulster Rifles

The Battalion wore two types of cap badge, the first, the harp topped with a king's crown and the motto QUIS SEPARABIT on the bottom, white metal for other ranks. The NCOs and officers wore the second type, a harp with a king's crown and a scroll through the middle which read ROYAL ULSTER RIFLES and came in white metal or silver.

The 1st title was dark green with black lettering ROYAL ULSTER RIFLES. This was worn until mid-1942, after which the second title was worn. This was light blue ROYAL ULSTER RIFLES on a dark blue background and was discontinued in December 1943. After this date they reverted to the black on green title.

1st Airborne Division

The Division was formed on 15 December, 1941. It then consisted of the 1st Parachute Brigade and the 1st Air-Landing Brigade.

Divisional Troops
458 Independent Light Battery RA was reassigned 1st Air-Landing Light Battery RA on 27 July, 1942.

31st Independent Reconnaissance Company became 1st Airborne Reconnaissance Squadron on 28 April, 1942.

31st Independent Infantry Brigade Company RASC became 1st Airborne Composite Company RASC on 7 August, 1942.

261 Field Park Company RE.

1st Airborne Divisional Signals formed in April, 1942.

1st Airborne Divisional Postal Unit formed in May, 1942.

1st Air-landing Anti-Tank Battery RA (re-designated from 223 Anti-Tank battery RA). Formed in June, 1942.

1st Airborne Division Provost Company (formed around 1 Air-Landing Brigade Group Provost Section).

21st Independent Parachute Company formed in July, 1942.

Light Tank Squadron (converted from Special B and C Service Light Tank Squadron) formed in August 1942.

2nd Air-landing Anti-Tank Battery RA (re-designated from 204 Anti-Tank Battery RA) formed in September 1942.

HQ RA Airborne Division, formed in October 1942.

127 Parachute Field Ambulance, formed in December 1942.

1st Airborne Light Tank Squadron, formed May 1943.

224th Field Ambulance formed 224th Parachute Field Ambulance RAMC in November, 1942.

1st Air Landing Anti-aircraft Battery, 1942-44.

Insignia

The 133rd and 224th Parachute Field Ambulance wore an unofficial title PARACHUTE with the letters R.A.M.C. white on maroon. This was short-lived and they reverted to the R.A.M.C. shoulder title. The first Air-Landing Anti-aircraft Battery wore the title ROUGH RIDERS, light blue on purple. This is because the unit started life as the 283 Light Anti-aircraft Battery (City of London Yeomanry T A) RA. They wore this title for only two years.

1st Air-Landing Anti-Tank Battery

Wore the title ANTI TANK BATTERY red on dark blue, from mid 1941 onwards.

2nd Air-Landing Anti-Tank Battery

Wore the title ANTI-TANK ARTILLERY red on dark blue, from mid-1941 onwards.

The 458th Independent Light Battery wore the title THE LIGHT ARTILLERY, in yellow on black for a period of fourteen months.

The 1st Air Landing Reconnaissance Squadron just wore the shoulder title RECONNAISSANCE in yellow on green. The cap badge was the normal Reconnaissance cap badge consisting of a spear flanked by forked lightning above a scroll which said RECONNAISSANCE CORPS. It was white metal for other ranks and silver or silver and gilt for officers.

6th Airborne Division

This Division began to form in the late summer of 1943 and consisted of the 3rd and 5th Parachute Brigades and 6th Air-Landing Brigade.

Divisional Troops
Royal Army Service Corps
Royal Army Pay Corps
Royal Electrical and Mechanical Engineers
Army Physical Training Corps
3rd Hussars (1945 onwards).

6th Airborne Armoured Reconnaissance Regiment
It was formed in 1941 as Special B and C Service Light Tank Squadron and was converted in August 1942 to the Airborne Light Tank Squadron. Volunteers from the Royal Tank Regt augmented this. They were sent for training in the Tetrarch Airborne Tank Carrier in the large Hamilcar glider. In May 1943 it joined 6th Airborne and became First Airborne Light Tank Squadron. Then in January 1944

it became the 6th Airborne Armoured Reconnaissance Regiment. Its numbers were augmented by men from three more regiments: 2nd Dragoon Guards, 9th Lancers and 10th Hussars.

Insignia

The cap badge was a white metal version of the regular Reconnaissance badge but the officers wore two variations, silver and gilt or silver. These were worn either in the beret or the side cap.

The collar badge was a smaller version of the cap badge. Again it came in white metal for all other ranks and silver or silver and gilt for officers. (It was not unusual for the officers to wear their collar badge in their red berets.) When they were known as the Light Tank Squadron they wore the shoulder title LIGHT TANK SQUADRON in yellow on a red background. By 1943 this had changed to the standard RECONNAISSANCE CORPS shoulder title of yellow on green.

6th Air-Landing Brigade

Formed at the same time as 6 Airborne Division, by the time the Brigade went into action in Normandy in 1944, it had been joined by the 1st Battalion Ulster Rifles and 2nd Battalion Oxfordshire and Buckinghamshire Light Infantry from 1st Air-Landing Brigade. Its third battalion was:

12th Battalion Devonshire Regiment

They began the war as the 50th Battalion and then were formed into the 12th (Holding) Battalion. In September 1943 they joined the Air-Landing Brigade. The shoulder title was white lettering DEVON on a red background.

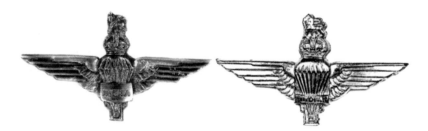

Airborne Units Of The Indian Army

50th (Indian) Parachute Brigade

Formed in Delhi on 10 October 1941, and was made up of the following units:

50th Indian Parachute Brigade Signal Section.
151 Parachute Battalion, which was made up of volunteers from twenty-three British Infantry battalions then stationed in India.

152 Indian Parachute Battalion.

153 Gurkha Parachute Battalion was formed from volunteers from nine Gurkha regiments.

411 (Royal Bombay) Parachute Section Indian Engineers.

In 1942 151 Battalion was transferred to the Middle East to join the 4th Parachute Brigade and was re-numbered 156 Parachute Battalion.

In December 1942 the 3rd Battalion, 7th Gurkha Rifles arrived to take their place and in early 1943 were changed to 154 Gurkha Parachute Battalion.

In October 1944 it was decided to enlarge the Indian Airborne into a division, to be known as the 9th Indian Airborne Division but was later reassigned the title 44th Indian Airborne Division.

44th Indian Airborne Division

50th (Indian) Parachute Brigade

16th (British) Parachute Battalion 1st (Indian) Parachute Battalion which was formed from 152 Parachute Battalion.

3rd (Gurkha) Parachute Battalion formed from 154 Parachute Battalion.

77th (Indian) Parachute Brigade

15th (British) Parachute Battalion.

4th (Indian) Parachute Battalion formed from 152 Parachute Battalion.

2nd (Gurkha) Parachute Battalion formed from 153 Parachute Battalion.

44th (British) Independent Pathfinder Company.

14th Air-Landing Brigade.

2nd Battalion Black Watch.

4th Rajputana Rifles (Outram's).

6th/16th Punjab Regiment.

Recce

44th Indian Airborne Division Recce Squadron (Governor General's Bodyguard).

Royal Artillery

159 Parachute Light Regiment RA 23rd LA/ATk Regt RA.

Royal Engineers

40th Indian Field Park Squadron.

33rd Parachute Squadron Indian Engineers.

411 Parachute Squadron Indian Engineers.

12th Parachute Squadron Royal Engineers which was made up of special forces, i.e. Chindits etc.

Robert Giles 44th Indian Airborne Division 1945.

Royal Indian Army Service Corps
Parachute Supply Company.
610 Airborne Light (Jeep) Company.
604 Airborne J.T. Company.
165th Airborne J.T. Company.

Indian Army Medical Corps/Indian Medical Service
7th Indian Parachute Field Ambulance.
80th Indian Parachute Field Ambulance.
60th Indian Parachute Field Ambulance.

Indian Electrical Mechanical Engineers
44th Indian Airborne Division Workshop.

Insignia
Insignia for the Indian Airborne is a very emotive subject. There is a large amount of insignia of various types but little in the way of information about who wore what or why.

The first set of insignia worn by 151 Battalion was on their bush hat. It was a rectangle or square in blue with a white parachute. On their epaulettes they wore a metal shoulder title 151. As 151, they had

their own wing which was a white parachute with blue wings on a black background. In early 1943, when the battalion was sent to the Middle East, they were reassigned as the 156th and were no longer part of the Indian Army but for some reason they kept their special wing. They wore their special badge only on their bush hats and the standard parachute badge in their red berets.

152 Battalion wore a maroon diamond with a white parachute in the centre which was worn on their bush hat. There is also found a badge which is triangular with a white parachute above a Vickers machine gun in black. This was believed to be worn on the sleeve by the Heavy Machine Gun Section of that unit. On their epaulette they wore the shoulder title 152 in brass.

153 Battalion had a white parachute and a pair of crossed kukris facing outwards, in white on a blue rectangle. It is not certain if

Instructors at Chaklala, India, February 1943.

15th Parachute Battalion, 1945.

Dutch parachute badges.

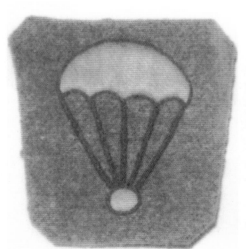

Italian Squadron F, 1943.

Australian wing.

153 wore a metal shoulder title but it seems likely that, as the other three battalions wore a title, these did as well.

154 Battalion had a white parachute with crossed kukris swept upwards, in white on dark rifle green.

Wings

As with 151, the other three battalions wore a similar wing. In photographic evidence, the wing was also worn on a side cap. The reason for this is unknown but it is believed that some of the European NCOs serving in this unit did so unofficially. The wing comes in a number of sizes and variations.

On the formation of the 44th Indian Airborne Division and the newly formed Indian Parachute Regiment, all adopted the new insignia with the exception of the two British Parachute Battalions; eventually, even they began to wear the new insignia. The badge was the standard parachute cap badge with the word INDIA on a tablet near the bottom of the badge. It came in cast silver, H M silver and die-cast white metal. They also adopted the Pegasus patch with the word INDIA. This was light blue on maroon. At this time, a variety of wings seemed to be adopted. Though the British parachute battalions wore the standard parachute badge, they did adopt the Pegasus INDIA.

The Air Landing Brigade wore a similar glider badge as the ones in 1st and 6th Airborne Division but instead of a blue glider it was deep red.

The Indian parachute field ambulance wore a white parachute on medical colours.

In this chapter I have also shown examples of foreign wings: for example, the French and Dutch paratroopers, Squadron F Italian paratroopers post-1943, who served with the British Airborne. I have not gone into too much detail, as this could be a book in its own right.

Free French parachute wing.

THE AUSTRALIAN PARACHUTE BATTALION

This was formed in August, 1943, and although it did not go into action as a unit, it did provide a large number of trained parachutists for other operations, especially in the South-West Pacific.

Insignia

This unit wore the same as other airborne forces, Pegasus, straight AIRBORNE, etc. However, they had their own special wing which was light blue on maroon.

The shoulder title AUSTRALIA was dark blue on a light blue slip-on.

Z SPECIAL UNIT

This was an Australian unit which was so secret that it was known only to the Prime Minister and the High Command. In 1942 John Curtin, then Prime Minister of Australia, approved the setting up of a unit which would undertake espionage in enemy-occupied territory. The unit was directly responsible to the Australian Commander in Chief, General Blarney. The unit was an off-shoot of the British SOE and had various names until the cover name of Special Reconnaissance Department (SRD) was decided upon. Its job was to cause as much trouble behind enemy lines as possible, attack shipping and organize local resistance, as well as supply intelligence reports to make it possible for the 9th Australian Division to attack Japanese-held areas. Most of the troops were Australian but it also included British, New Zealand, Canadian, US, Dutch, Portuguese, Chinese, Free French, Malay, Timorese and Philippines, plus local natives from Japanese occupied areas.

Units within the force were:

M Special Unit – Coast Watchers – some New Zealanders served in this
Far Eastern Liaison Office – FELO
Special Duties Flight 200 (RAAF)
Secret Intelligence Australia – SIA
Netherlands Forces Intelligence Section NEFI Div.(lll)
Philippine Regional Section – PRS
Allied Translator and Interpreter Section – ATIS

Members of this unit were specially selected and had to volunteer for each operation. They worked either alone or in pairs. 380 agents were inserted behind Japanese lines; of these, seventy-eight were parachuted into action and the rest went by submarine, boat, US PT boat or small aircraft. Around 260 operations were undertaken. Many of those who were captured were tortured and beheaded.

They had no special insignia. If they had received parachute training in Australia they were allowed to wear Australian parachute wings on their right sleeve; if they had been on active service, the wing was moved to the left breast.

The Canadian Parachute Battalion

This was formed in July, 1942, from Canadian forces in the UK. Later, it was enhanced by a large group of volunteers from Canada who were trained first in the USA (at Fort Benning), then in Canada (at Shilo) and finally in England where they had to undergo a conversion course as they had been trained by American methods with American equipment. In 1943 the unit was placed under the command of the 6th Airborne Division and the Battalion arrived in the UK in July. The unit served with the 6th Airborne Division in the D-Day Normandy landings and pursued the retreating Germans across the Rhine back into Germany. After their return from Germany to the UK in May 1945 they were the first Canadian unit to be repatriated.

English made

Canadian made

First issued February 1944

English made

English made

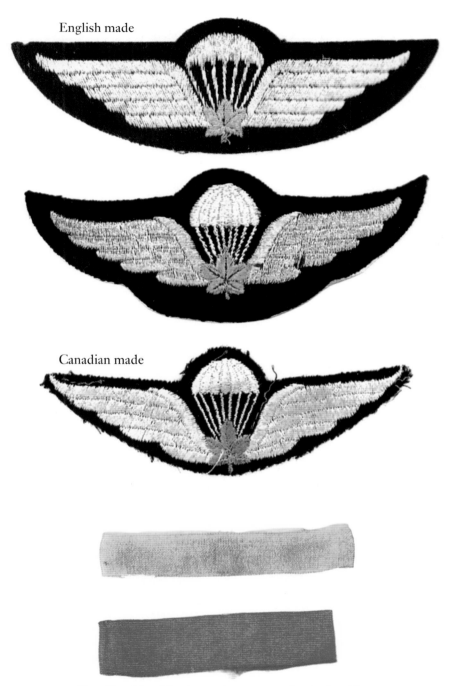

Canadian made

Battalion identification strips worn on both shoulders
around the shoulder straps from October 1943.

Insignia

Their first badge was in plastic and was chocolate-coloured; the officers wore a larger version of the same badge. Then the brass version was issued with the officers' version being in silver and gilt. The cap badge was a silver parachute with two gilt wings rising vertically from a silver scroll on which was written CANADIAN PARACHUTE CORPS. There is a Canadian maker as well as an English maker of the officers' badges.

English made and issued in 1943.

The collar badges were worn by the officers only and were in silver and gilt, again made by both English and Canadian makers. The design is a cloud with the words EX COELIS, from which comes a hand holding a dagger.

The shoulder title came in two variations; the first one authorized in April, 1943, is AIRBORNE CANADA, white on dark green and then the other which was worn from D Day onwards, said 1 CANADIAN PARACHUTE BATTALION. It comes in both printed and woven variations. There are at least three versions of the woven variation.

Corporal F. G. Thopham VC.

OR's badge on red beret.

Bakelite cap badge.

English made bullion wing.

Parachute Jump Instructors – Royal Air Force

All parachute training came under the auspices of the
RAF. When the Parachute Regiment was formed the
RAF was given the task of training the men and to
train instructors from other units but the whole
training scheme came under the RAF.

Insignia

The badge consisted of a parachute surrounded by a
wreath in blue grey for ordinary wear, and in red for
tropical service dress. It is also known that instructors in
India wore a white parachute and blue laurel leaf on a grey background; it was worn
on the right sleeve above the chevrons, and it is also worn on a light blue brassard.
Officially approved in May, 1943, but was unofficially worn from as early as 1941.

RAF liason officer at Tito's headquarters, Yugoslavia, 1944. Note the RAF jump wing on upper right arm.

Sergeant Yexley Parachute jump instructor at Chaklala, India, 1943.

1st Polish Independent Parachute Brigade

Parachuting had been a popular pastime of Polish youth organizations and so the beginnings of a parachute force with its own training centre was already in existence before Poland was invaded in 1939.

The brigade owed its origins to the 4th Cadre Rifle Brigade which had been formed in August, 1940, from the Canadian Rifle Brigade. This brigade had been formed a few months previously in Scotland from the remnants of the 4th Infantry Division which had been evacuated to England after the fall of France. Originally, it had been intended that the Canadian Rifle Brigade should be sent to Canada in order to train volunteers for the Polish forces; instead, it was renamed and remained in England where volunteers were trained as secret agents for operations in Poland.

During that winter, Colonel Sosabowski, the Brigade Commander borrowed ski equipment from the Norwegians and introduced skiing courses for his men. In January 1941 the Polish Headquarters suggested that Sosabowski's men should undertake parachute training. This was done in Manchester and from then on the idea of a Polish parachute division developed. Sosabowski was not completely satisfied with the training his men received and subsequently, they returned to Scotland where they set up their own training school and in addition helped in the parachute training of other special units. The Parachute Brigade came into existence on 9 October, 1941.

Polish paratrooper with a homing pigeon, used for back-up communication.

It had been planned that the brigade should be used for operations in Poland but in early 1944 the Polish authorities agreed it could be used elsewhere and thus it became part of Operation MARKET GARDEN and took part in the battle for Arnhem. There, it was proposed that the Polish Brigade, in three groups, would land on the south bank of the river which it would later cross after the British had captured Arnhem Bridge. As is well documented,

Major General S. Sosabowski.

Arnhem was 'a bridge too far' and this part of the entire operation ran into difficulties. The Poles suffered 500 casualties. After Arnhem, some of the Polish Brigade was employed guarding airfields and then in mid-October, they were sent to Ostende from where they were shipped back to the UK and billeted near Peterborough.

Back in the UK, the Brigade was reorganized and new recruits were trained. In May, 1945, they returned to mainland Europe where they were under the command of the 1st Polish Armoured Division and operated alongside the British Army of the Rhine until disbanded in the area of Osnabruck, Germany, 19 May, 1947.

Brigade commanders:

23–Sep–41	Colonel	S. Sosabowski
15–Jun–44	Major General	S. Sosabowski
27–Dec–44	Lieutenant Colonel	S. Jachnik
Mar–45	Major	Tonn (temporary)
13–Apr–45	Colonel	A. Szczerbo-Rawicz

Brigade Troops

Artillery
Anti-tank Batteries Airborne Anti-Tank Battery (1942–47) Light Batteries
Airborne Light Artillery Battery (1942–47) not at Arnhem due to shortage of gliders

Engineers
Field Companies
Airborne Engineer Company (1942–47)

Medical
Parachute Medical Company 1942–47

Signals
Airborne Signals Company (1942–47)

Supply & Transport
Airborne Transport and Supply Company (May–42 May–47)

Units:

1st Polish Parachute Infantry Battalion	23–Sep–41 19–May–47
2nd Polish Parachute Infantry Battalion	23–Sep–41 19–May–47
3rd Polish Parachute Infantry Battalion	23–Sep–41 19–May–47
4th Polish Parachute Infantry Battalion	Feb–44 Mar–44

    broken up to reinforce other battalions in Mar–44

The first wing worn by the Polish paratroopers was given by the parachute manufacturers, GQ Parachute Company. Shown left being worn above the left breast pocket.

Higher Formations served under:

HQ Polish Forces in Britain	23-Sep-41 Apr-44
1 British Airborne Corps	Apr-44 10-Aug-44
1 Airborne Division	10-Aug-44 29-Sep-44
1 British Airborne Corps	29-Sep-44 04-Nov-44
1 Airborne Division	04-Nov-44 08-May-45
1 British Corps 08-May-45	29-Jun-45
1 Polish Armoured Division	29-Jun-45 19-May-47

Theatres

United Kingdom	23-Sep-41 21-Sep-44
Netherlands	21-Sep-44 07-Oct-44
Belgium	07-Oct-44 11-Oct-44
United Kingdom	11-Oct-44 08-May-45
Germany	08-May-45 19-May-47
Belgium	08-May-45

Chapter 6

Special Operations Executive (SOE)

SOE was formed in 1940 with the intention of encouraging and working with resistance forces in Europe. Poland was its first area of operations. Its operatives were expected to advocate and support resistance in Occupied Europe. Many of these operatives were recruited from branches of the services and as such retained their original uniform and rank. Female members were commissioned into the FANYs or WAAFs. SOE had its fingers in many pies from France to Poland, Egypt to Yugoslavia and India to South-East Asia.

The work of SOE, MI5 and MI6 in America was organized from New York by William Stephenson, a Canadian who was a personal friend of Winston Churchill. He worked closely with William Donovan, thus enabling SOE and the American Office of Strategic Services (OSS), to cooperate closely.

Although OSS had tried to recruit linguists, very few Americans could manage to pass themselves off as French, so few were used in Europe until after the D–Day landings. It was after that event that the Jedburghs were used (see page 155).

Much of the work of SOE still remains secret, even to the numbers of personnel actually employed by them.

SOE was disbanded immediately after the war ended on the orders of Clement Atlee, the new Prime Minister.

Insignia

SOE wore no special insignia. Most of the men wore the service dress or battle–dress uniform of their parent unit i.e. Yorkshire Regiment, Scots Guards and so on. Those women who were FANYs, WAAFs or ATS wore their respective uniforms and insignia.

As most SOE operatives were parachute-trained, they wore the standard parachute wing. It has been claimed that they wore a special wing just for SOE but there is no evidence, photographic or otherwise, to support this.

Force 136

This was a branch of SOE which was involved in guerrilla activities in Malaya, Burma, Siam, French Indo-China, Java, Sumatra, Timor and Sarawak. They were transported and serviced by the Special Duties Squadrons of the RAF and by Royal Navy submarines (see also Jedburghs, page 156).

Insignia
They wore a distinctive metal wing and some unusual, locally-made wings.

Men of Force 136.

The Jedburghs

The Jedburghs were named after guerrillas who had operated in Scotland in the twelfth century. Most received their training in Britain. They comprised teams of three who would join up with local resistance groups, organize, equip and provide them with W/T communications and generally act as a focal point for local resistance. Each three-man team was intended to consist of one British or American officer with one W/T operator and a national of the country of operation, although this was not always the case; in fact, only ten of the teams were so mixed.

There were fifty-five British Jedburghs, drawn from the KRR, the Buffs, the Black Watch, the Royal Welch Fusiliers and the Camerons, among others, with no two coming from the same regiment. Some went in alongside SAS units and four were with the airborne at Arnhem and Nijmegen. Between June, 1944, and May, 1945, the Jedburghs carried out 101 operations in France and Holland. After victory in Europe, many British Jedburghs joined Force 136 where they carried out thirty operations behind enemy lines in Malaya and Burma; some American Jedburghs joined the Special Allied Reconnaissance Force (see page 159).

Insignia

Jedburghs wore a variety of insignia. First, was the SF (Special Forces) wing. This was a white wing with a red circle in the centre with blue letters SF in the centre on a black background, in cloth. They also wore a metal wing with a star at the bottom of the canopy. This was made out of a Parachute Regiment cap badge which had the wings clipped and the crown removed from the top of the canopy and replaced with a large brass star.

In addition, some men wore their own country's parachute wings i.e. the French, Poles and British. In some cases, personnel wore three wings, i.e. the Poles who wore the Polish wing over their left breast pocket, the British wing over their right pocket and the SF wing on their left or right sleeve.

The Americans wore only their wing on the upper part of the sleeve but it could be worn on either side.

R Force

This force was made up of 1240 men who came mainly from the Royal Engineers and Royal Signals. It was the deception unit of the British 21st Army Group. Its task was to deceive the Germans into believing that the D Day landings of June, 1944 were to take place somewhere other than Normandy. Their deceit was sufficiently successful to keep the German 15th Army occupied for weeks in the Pas de Calais and by the time they realized their mistake it was too late. In 1945 they were also

Members of the Jedburgh force. (Courtesy of Les Hughes USA)

able to trick the Germans into believing that a much larger force of men and tanks was preparing to cross the Rhine. They used rubber and cardboard cutouts as guns, tanks and landing craft, as well as sound effects. The force was disbanded just before the end of the war.

Insignia

The Badge

As this unit was made up chiefly of Royal Signals and Royal Engineers, it was decided that they should wear their own cap badges. It was also decided that R Force was to wear a shoulder patch which came in two variations. The first was a white R on a black shield which the men of the Royal Signals supposedly wore; the second was a white R on a blue square which, supposedly, the men of the Royal Engineers wore.

Phantom

This group was formed in October, 1939, as part of No.3 British Air Mission in France and originally comprised only four personnel. Its commanding officer was Lieutenant Colonel Hopkinson. It was formed to get important information from the battlefield to the Commander-in-Chief as quickly as possible. Its first

mission was to pass on the positions of Belgian and German troops should the Germans invade. This would enable Air Striking Force Headquarters to determine where to bomb. Hopkinson realized that a specially trained force would be needed to do the job efficiently as its operatives would need to be highly mobile as well as capable of transmitting their information accurately and speedily to both the RAF as well as the C-in-C Land Forces. Within a month, Hopkinson had recruited a small group of armoured car troops from the 12th Lancers. At first there was a problem about an Army unit, however small, servicing the RAF. Eventually, this matter was resolved and the name Phantom was given to the unit. Men from the Royal Tank Regiment replaced the Lancers and Queen Victoria's Rifles, plus a few from Signals.

Insignia

This was a white letter P on a black square. It was worn on the top part of the shoulder.

The Special Allied Airborne Reconnaissance Force

The Force officially came into being in March, 1945, although ideas for it had been mooted as far back as 1943. Its task was to try to ensure the safety of prisoners of war and slave workers once the enemy realized that the war was lost. Each team would parachute behind enemy lines, enter prison camps and intimidate the commandant until the Allied armies arrived. The Force was formed at great speed and it was expected that 120 teams of three would be ready by the middle of April. Recruits came from the British SAS, American Jedburghs, SOE and OSS agents, French, Polish and Belgian paratroopers. By the required April deadline, only sixty teams were ready but they were thought to be needed so desperately that they were dispatched immediately across the channel to the 6th US Army Group Headquarters. Once there, however, they found that they were not even expected.

The Force took part in just one airborne assignment, at the end of April, 1945, when six teams were dropped around the area occupied by Stalag XI which housed 20,000 Allied prisoners. Four of the teams, British and American, were captured almost immediately, becoming captives themselves in the camp they had come to 'liberate'. One of the French teams was dropped in the middle of an enemy division but managed to get away, only to be captured later by the Russians; two members of the second French team disappeared without trace. The Force was disbanded at the end of June that year, having been in existence for little over seven weeks.

Insignia
The Force wore the shoulder title S.A.A.R.F. in yellow on a black background. This comes in printed and woven examples. Its members wore a white wing with a red arrow at its base, on an airforce blue background. On the bottom of the wing there was a circle of red chains. The wing could be worn on the upper left shoulder but the Americans preferred to wear it on the lower part of the right sleeve. It was not uncommon for the men of S.A.A.R.F to wear other parachute wings as well.

The Women's Transport Service (FANY)

The First Aid Nursing Yeomanry was founded by Regimental Sergeant Major Baker, who initially thought of the idea in 1898 when serving during Kitchener's Sudan campaign. As a result of his experiences there, he realized that those wounded on the battlefield stood a better chance of survival if they received immediate medical help as, by the time the slow-moving field ambulances reached them, many had died of their wounds. The idea was to train a small force of volunteer horsewomen whose job was to ride around the battlefield and provide speedy first aid to the wounded.

Mixed nationalities of SAARF. Left to right: two British, two French, two American and two Polish. (Courtesy of Les Hughes USA)

Margaret Pawley FANY (SOE).
(Reproduced from her memoirs in
Obedience to Instructions, Leo Cooper,
1999)

When Baker left the army he decided to recruit such a force and to this end advertised in newspapers in 1907.

At a time when a lot of women were seeking to prove themselves men's equals, many rushed to join this unit. The First Aid Nursing Yeomanry was registered in July, 1909, and by the outbreak of the First World War was a disciplined and well-drilled force of horsewomen ready to tend wounded soldiers where they fell. However, trench warfare rendered their skills redundant and instead they became stretcher-bearers. Nevertheless, the British Army decided it had no use for them in this capacity, although the Belgian Army welcomed them and for most of the war, the FANYs served with Belgian and French units.

Yet, by 1917, the War Office and the British Red Cross Society were determined not to allow British women to serve in Flanders unless they were affiliated to them. The proposal was to abolish the FANYs. It was only intervention from the Belgian Army which prevented this but it was not until 1927 that the FANYs were given official recognition. They were named in the Army List as a voluntary reserve transport unit and shortly before the Second World War their name became the Women's Transport Service although they were referred to as the 'Fannies'.

Even during the Second World War, efforts were made to disperse the unit by merging them with the ATS. By a lucky chance, two FANYs were chosen to pack supplies and explosives for secret sabotage operations in 1940 and from then onwards, the unit became synonymous with the Special Operations Executive. The women in this unit trained secret agents to pose as typists and clerks, orderlies, and drivers; they sent and received coded messages to and from these agents; some FANYs became secret agents themselves. Many were captured, tortured and killed and of these, three won the George Cross and two the George Medal. One FANY served with the early Commandos and Nancy March-Phillipps, who was the wife of the commander of the small scale raiding force, became the only woman to serve in the unit and to wear the SAS wings.

Insignia

The cap badge is a bronze circle with a plain cross in the centre, and the words Women's Transport Service (FANY) around the edge of the circle. The collar badges were exact copies of the cap badge but half the size, and worn on a maroon background. The WTS (Women's Transport Service) shoulder title has red letters on light khaki; some SOE recruits had the initials F.A.N.Y in blue letters on maroon.

Chapter 7

United States Airborne and Raiding Forces

82 US Airborne Division

This formation started life in the First World War as the 82 All American Infantry Division. It was mobilized in March, 1942, and in August became the 82 Airborne Division. It first saw action in North Africa in April, 1943, and took part in the Sicily landings of that year as well as the 1944 Arnhem-Nijmegen operations and the Battle of the Ardennes.

Insignia
This was a two-part patch. The top part was a curved scroll with the word AIRBORNE, white on blue. The bottom part was a square in red with a blue circle in the centre with the letters AA in white.

US parachute wing worn above left breast pocket.

101 US Airborne Division

The Division was formed from a nucleus of the 82 Airborne in August 1942. It sailed for England in September, 1943. Early in 1944 General Maxwell Taylor took over command. The 101st was part of the invasion force for D Day. It was their job to jump in before the seaborne forces arrived to secure the beach-head. After thirty-three days of fighting they were relieved and returned to England to train for their next mission, Operation MARKET GARDEN, to seize the bridges over the Rhine, cross the river at Arnhem and then march into Germany. After seventy-two days in combat, the Division was relieved at the end of November. In the middle of December they received orders to proceed to Bastogne and became involved in the defence of the town during the German offensive in the Ardennes. They were relieved by the arrival of the 4th Armoured Division. For this defence they received the Distinguished Unit Citation. Their last

Major General Jim Gavin, Commanding General of the 82nd Airborne Division, January 1945.

Worn on the side cap.

General Maxwell Taylor commanding officer 101st Airborne.

National Flag worn by American
Special Forces during opening phases
of assaults against enemy-held territory.

mission of the war was the capture
of Hitler's retreat at Berchtesgaden.
The division was de-activated in
November, 1945.

Insignia
This was a black shield with the
head of an American bald eagle in
white and yellow with a scroll over
the shield saying AIRBORNE.

The Rangers

1st Ranger Battalion and Darby's Rangers

Rangers was the name given to the USA's commando-type troops.

The 1st Battalion was formed from US troops stationed in Northern Ireland in June, 1942. After training, they were sent to Algeria in November (codename, Operation TORCH) to capture the port of Oran. They were commanded by William Darby and for most of their existence were known as Darby's Rangers.

After the capture of Oran, the Rangers underwent further training, especially in night fighting. Their next assault, much of it done at night, was a raid in the foothills of the Sened Pass; this was also successful. Several enemy cannon and machine guns were destroyed and useful intelligence was gained from German and Italian prisoners. The Rangers fought further battles in North Africa but were withdrawn in March, 1943.

William Darby, commanding officer of the 1st Ranger Battalion.

In October, 1943, the three Ranger Battalions landed at Salerno in Italy where they spent forty-five days in the field and suffered 40 per cent casualties. They were re-organized for the Anzio landings in January, 1944, where the 1st and 3rd Battalions suffered 60 per cent casualties. Of the survivors, only eighteen escaped capture.

2nd Ranger Battalion
The Battalion was formed in the USA in April, 1943. They were part of the D Day landings of 1944 and fought for two days before they were relieved. Although successful, they suffered heavy losses. After reinforcements were trained, their next action was to protect the US 29th Division in the attack on Brest. When the Conquet peninsular was taken, the Rangers moved on to Paris, then Luxembourg and reached Germany by December, 1944. At the beginning of 1945 they moved further east, eventually into Czechoslovakia. The Battalion was disbanded in June 1945.

3rd Ranger Battalion
This was formed in North Africa from volunteers, mainly from the 1st Battalion. Their first action was in Sicily in July, 1943, and in September they reached the mainland of Italy, landing at Salerno. In January, 1944, they were in action in Anzio.

4th Ranger Battalion
They were formed in April, 1943, and saw action with the 1st and 3rd Rangers in Italy. The Battalion was disbanded after the Anzio campaign and the remnants of the 1st, 3rd and 4th Rangers were transferred into the First Special Service Force.

5th Ranger Battalion
They were formed in late 1943 in the United States and took part in the D Day landings in Normandy in June, 1944, for which action they received a Presidential Citation. They took part in the action with the 2nd Rangers in Brest and in October and November provided the security at Headquarters 12th Army Group in Belgium. In December they were attached to the Sixth Cavalry Group of General Patton's Third Army. In February, 1945 they were attached to the 94th Infantry Division to secure the bridgehead across the River Roer. In April they took 1000 Germans to see Buchenwald Concentration Camp and later that month, they took one of the bridges across the Danube. They were disbanded in June, 1945.

Rangers training for D-Day 1 June 1944.

6th Ranger Battalion

This Battalion was formed in August, 1944, in New Guinea from the 98th Field Artillery Battalion. They were in action three days before the main force's Philippine landings in October, 1944. They were involved in the landings on Luzon in January, 1945, and soon afterwards rescued American prisoners from behind enemy lines, for which action every man was decorated. Later, they marched 250 miles in twenty-eight days behind enemy lines to prepare the landing zones for the paratroopers to land in the last operation in the Philippines. They were disbanded in Japan in December, 1945.

Insignia

The Rangers wore a shoulder title of a scroll pattern with the letters RANGER BN prefixed with the Battalion's number. The numbers and letters were in white edged with a red border on a black background. On D-Day they wore the shoulder patch RANGER in gold on a blue diamond with gold edgings.

First title worn by men training in Northern Ireland in 1942.

Second Ranger Battalion men near Rhurberg, Germany 1945.

Brigadier General Robert T. Frederick (with binoculars) with
Lieutenant Colonel Robert S. Moore at Anzio 1944, wearing the
First Special Service Force patch.

First Special Service Force

The idea for this force originated with the British who, unfortunately, lacked the
manpower and special industrial capacity to manufacture the special equipment
required in a short time. Therefore, the plan, codenamed Operation PLOUGH was
passed to the Americans. The unit was formed in 1942 under the command of
Lieutenant Colonel Robert Frederick. Initially, it was intended to be made up of one
third Americans, one third Canadians and one third Norwegians but this soon
became half Americans and half Canadians. The unit was chosen from volunteers
from all parts of the American Army and from Canadian units at home or in Britain;
the two nationalities were completely integrated within the force.

They were intended to be a sabotage unit and their first objective was to be the
heavy water plant at Rjukan and various hydro–electric installations in Norway.
However, in spite of extensive training, during which they had learnt to parachute,
ski, climb mountains and make amphibious raids, Operation PLOUGH was
cancelled.

The force first went into action in August, 1943, to lead the initial invasion of
Kiska in the Aleutian Islands only to find that the Japanese had evacuated the island
three days previously. The force was immediately recalled to San Francisco.

In December, they were in Italy. They made a two–night climb of La Difensa's
cliffs which the Germans had considered unassailable and took the top of the hill

within two hours. The fighting continued for three days during which the force had suffered significant losses. Nevertheless, they were back in the front line within eleven days. Their next assignment was to protect a drive down Highway 6. The force fought deep into the Italian hills and was withdrawn by the middle of January 1944; their numbers had been reduced to only 25 per cent of their original number. Two weeks later they were at Anzio where they earned their nickname of the 'Black Devils' as a result of blackening their faces before a raid; the majority of their raids there were at night. They took over the Mussolini Canal forcing back the German line. During the Anzio campaign they lost about a third of their number but reinforcements replaced them; some of these came from survivors of the Rangers raid on Cisterna; others came from Canada.

The force worked its way towards Rome and entered the city on 4 June, 1944; it was their task to secure all eight bridges over the River Tiber.

After the fall of Rome, the force was transferred to the 7th Army and initiated the invasion of southern France on the Hyeres Islands. They chased the Germans through France, as far as the Italian border. They were relieved at the end of November, 1944, and disbanded in the following month.

Insignia
The unit wore a variety of insignia. The first was the famous patch which was a spearhead shaped in red with white lettering USA horizontally across the top and with the word CANADA vertically down the middle. The second was the oval to the wing which was red, white and blue with two machine holes at either side so that the metal wing could be placed on it. The shoulder title read 2ND.REG. Black Devils F.S.S.F in white on red. This also comes in bullion. On the collar they wore crossed arrows in metal or, for No. 1 dress, in bullion.

The metal wing was the same as that worn by US paratroopers. It is also known that members of the Canadian section wore the Canadian wing.

Merrill's Marauders

Officially this unit was the 5307th Composite Unit (Provisional) but soon became known as Merrill's Marauders after its commanding officer Brigadier General Frank Merrill. It was formed in January, 1944, from US volunteers stationed in the Pacific, Caribbean and America with the intention of being a long-range penetration unit in Burma. It owed its existence to the success of the Chindits plus Orde Wingate's

persuasive arguments at the Washington Conference of senior Allied commanders about the need to broaden and increase the role of his Chindits in Burma. It consisted of nearly 3000 personnel and the codename of their operation was 'Galahad'.

The force's first objective was to strike at the Japanese supply lines and their first attack on Walawbum was successful. Two subsequent, simultaneous attacks were met with fierce resistance from the enemy with the result that the Marauders were forced to withdraw and the battalions were unable to support each other.

The 2nd Battalion had been forced to withdraw to Nhpum Ga where they were besieged for eleven days during which time the men endured almost unbearable conditions from the intense heat and humidity, flies, leeches and sickness; then there was the stench from decomposing waste and mule bodies, not to mention the intense bombardment from the Japanese. The 3rd Battalion was eventually relieved and then tried to relieve the 2nd Battalion but it was not until reinforcements arrived in the guise of the 1st Battalion that they were able to do so.

After that, the weary force expected to be allowed time for rest and recuperation but that was not to be. Although they had lost around 700 men killed, wounded or sick and with no chance of replacements, they were ordered to seize the airfield at Myitkyina. This involved a sixty-five-mile march over the 6000 foot mountains of the Kumon Range to reach the airfield. Despite all odds, the Marauders and their Chinese allies reached the airfield on 17 May and seized it. However, the Japanese soon sent reinforcements to Myitkyina and the Marauders were besieged. By 25 May the Americans were exhausted and ill so that between 75 and 100 men each day needed to be evacuated from the airstrip. Of the original complement of Marauders, only 1,310 had actually reached Myitkyina and of these 679 had to be evacuated to hospital by 1 June. Hardly any of the remaining troops were fit for combat and of those few who were, there were not enough to form a fighting force. Therefore, the officers requested that the force be relieved. It was disbanded in August but not before it had received the Distinguished Unit Citation. During their short existence, the Marauders had fought five major and thirty smaller battles against the Japanese.

Around 200 men of the 1st Battalion remained to become the 475th Infantry which was combined with the 124th Cavalry, forming a new group, the Mars Task Force. Some others joined the Kachin guerrillas.

Insignia

There was no special insignia when the unit was first formed but a few badges of various descriptions are to be found near the end of its existence. The first was a shield quartered diagonally, with two blue and two green sections; in the top blue section was a sunburst in white; in the bottom blue section there was a white star; in the green sections was a red lightning bolt. Above the shield were the words MERRILL'S MARAUDERS in red. This was worn on their left shoulder and on the right shoulder they wore the China-Burma-India patch which is a shield with a white sunburst and a star on a dark blue background; this is sitting on red and white stripes.

General Frank D. Merrill with Lieutenant General
Joseph W. Stilwell, Burma, May 1944.

Mars Task Force

This force was made up of what was left of Merrill's Marauders, the 124th Cavalry and supporting units. They marched south and east through the mountains, attacking the Japanese where they could and by January, 1945, had reached the Burma Road. Aided by Kachin guerrillas, the Task Force cut the Japanese lines of communications forcing them to evacuate Lashio in March, thereby enabling the Allies to re-open the land route into China.

They then joined with Detachment 101 and by June, 1945, had driven the Japanese from the Taunggyi-Kentung region. Soon afterwards, the Americans joined the developing OSS groups in China.

Insignia

It seemed that because members of Merrill's Marauders formed a large part of the unit, they wore a similar badge but instead of Merrill's Marauders they added the words MARS TASK FORCE in red. When the force became the 475th Infantry it seems that the men kept the bottom half of the Merrill's badge but put a white edging all the way round the shield.

475th Infantry patch.

The Raiders

1st Raider Battalion

The Raider battalions were formed to provide hard-hitting assault troops who could make surprise, usually amphibious, hit and run attacks. The 1st Battalion was formed in February, 1942, and made its first assault against the Japanese in August, 1942, on Tulagi island at the same time as the 1st Marine Division attacked Guadalcanal. The Raiders then moved to Guadalcanal in September. In October they were withdrawn from the area.

Insignia

A blue shield with five white stars with a diamond in red in the centre of the shield in which was a white skull was common to all Raider units.

2nd Raider Battalion

They were formed around the same time as the First Raiders. They landed on Makin Island in August, 1942, where they wiped out the Japanese garrison. They also moved on to Guadalcanal where they operated for thirty-seven days behind enemy lines. In December they were withdrawn to Espiritu Santo.

3rd Raider Battalion

This battalion was formed in Samoa in September, 1942. Its first task was in January, 1943, to attack the Russell Islands which are east of Guadalcanal. In September, 1943, they joined the 2nd Battalion to form the 2nd Provisional Raider Regiment.

4th Raider Battalion

Formed in October, 1942, it was almost immediately joined with the 1st Raiders and two Army battalions to form the 1st Provisional Raider Regiment. In June, 1943, the 4th Raiders landed in new Georgia. In July the 1st Provisional Raider Regiment fought the battle of Bairko Harbour after which the Battalion withdrew to New Caledonia.

4th Marine Regiment

This was made up of the remnants of all four Raider Battalions in February, 1944. (The original 4th Marines had been lost at Corregidor.) In this new Regiment the 1st and 4th Raiders became the 1st and 2nd Battalions, the 3rd became the 3rd Battalion, while the 2nd Raiders was re-organized into the Regimental Weapons Company. The Regiment's first task was to take the island of Emirau. When they went ashore, they found that the Japanese had abandoned it.

Insignia
As for raiding units.

1st Provisional Brigade

This was formed on Guadalcanal in March, 1944, from two veteran regiments reinforced by other troops. They made their assault on the island of Guam in July, 1944. By the beginning of August, the island had been secured and the Brigade left shortly afterwards.

In September, 1944, the Brigade was re-designated the 6th Marine Division and in March, 1945, it sailed for Okinawa where a record number of the enemy were killed or captured after an assault lasting eighty-two days.

Insignia
This was a patch with a circle, red outer ring and blue centre. On the outer ring were the words Melanesia Star Micronesia Star Orient; in the middle, on the blue centre was a white sword superimposed on it.

2nd Marine Raider Regiment (Provisional)
This Regiment was formed in September, 1943, for operations on Bourgainville which lies between the two chains of the Solomon Islands. The occupying Japanese had a number of airfields there. The Raiders were withdrawn in January 1944, after a number of successful patrols against the Japanese and the Regiment was withdrawn and disbanded.

Chapter 8

Office of Strategic Services

This organization was formed in June, 1942, with Colonel William Donovan as its first director. It was the American version of SOE and its training was based on that of the British Commandos. It consisted of separate branches for intelligence (SI) and special operations (SO). The first groups were ready for action in the Mediterranean by early 1943. It was agreed that OSS would be responsible for operations in North-West Africa and the east coast of Asia while SOE was responsible elsewhere.

OSS carried out operations in, among other places, Tunisia (Darby's Rangers), Burma and China (Force 101, Jingpaw Rangers, Kachin Rangers and Merrill's Marauders), Holland and France (Jedburghs) with the Maquis.

It was disbanded in October, 1945.

Detachment 101 OSS

This was formed in 1942 from volunteers who had skills in demolition, medicine, communications and Asian cultures. Its leader was Captain Eifler. Although it was the brainchild of Colonel Donovan, the founder of OSS, it does not seem to have had the whole-hearted approval of General Stilwell who was in charge of operations in the China-Burma-India area. After training mainly in methods developed by SOE for European operations, the group left for the Far East in May only to find that they were not wanted and rather regarded with suspicion by America's Chinese allies. Eventually, it was agreed that they would collect information about what was happening in Burma. The Japanese occupation of that country had cut the Burma Road, the main supply line into China from the outside and Japanese aircraft were continually harassing American aircraft attempting to fly supplies into China. Local volunteers were recruited from refugees and these were divided into small groups. Detachment 101 trained Kachin guerrilla forces, who became known as the Kachin or Jingpaw Rangers. The newly constituted detachment was ready for operations by late 1942 or early 1943. However, problems still dogged their attempts as the Japanese managed to prevent all their efforts at infiltration and they had difficulties with the local British commander who tried to insist that he had control over all operations in his area. Fortunately, an arrangement was made between the detachment and Brigadier Alexander of Air Transport Command to help rescue any of his transport crews who came down in the jungle, where they stood little chance of survival among the Japanese forces, tigers and snakes. Friendly Kachin villagers could be organized into a network of rescuers and helpers who would guide them back to safety. This group was ready for action by February, 1943, and arrived back at its base at the end of May. It had been only partially successful. Unfortunately, the next two missions failed.

Gradually, the detachment's focus changed from sabotage to guerrilla warfare and their successes increased so that by 1944 several hundred guerrillas were deployed and there were a number of radio stations making regular reports from behind enemy lines. In addition, about 400 Allied aircrew had been rescued. In the end, detachment 101 and other special operations in the Far East played a most important role in defeating the Japanese.

It had been intended to disband the force once the Burma Road had been reached but it was requested that the Kachin Battalions be retained. Of these, 1500 volunteered for the advance south which was to be the final offensive. It was during this period that the heaviest losses were sustained, but by June they had driven the Japanese out of the Taunggyi-Kentung region for which they received the Distinguished Unit Citation. The detachment was de-activated in July 1945.

The OSS created an operational group in May 1943 to work in Yugoslavia, Burma and Italy to train the local partisans. The groups were Detachment 101 (Burma), 2667th OSS Regt. (Yugoslavia) and 2671st Special Reconnaissance Bn. (Italy).

Insignia
There is much debate about whether OSS and its close relation the Political Warfare Executive in SHAEF ever wore insignia – experts disagree on this matter (see Psychological Warfare Division below for description of badge).

The insignia for Detachment 101 was a silver bar with the words BURMA CAMPAIGN and in the centre, a circle with 101 above a flash of lightning.

The 2667th or the Third Contingent Operational Group was made up of Yugoslavian-speaking Americans who wore two badges (see Land Forces Adriatic for description). This group later became C Company of the 2671st Reconnaissance Battalion.

The 2671st wore a sleeve insignia in cloth which read SPECIAL RECON BN which is a golden-orange colour on black.

VETERAN INSIGNIA
In 1946 veterans wore a small metal lapel badge with the letters OSS in white on a red background.

Political Warfare Executive and Psychological Warfare Division

These were the names given to Britain's and America's army of propagandists whose role was to bring as much confusion and collapse of morale as possible to the enemy. The British end was formed in 1941 and had at first been part of SOE, but in a little over a year, became a separate unit. Among other things, it was this group which was responsible for the letter V (for victory) being used across Europe and its accompanying Morse sign, the opening notes of Beethoven's 5th Symphony. The Psychological Warfare Division was formed in 1944 to work with the PWE at SHAEF.

Insignia
This was a lapwing's head embroidered in black and white on a light blue diamond with a blue border. However, the American version of PWE, SHAEF's Psychological Warfare Division (OSS), wore a metal badge of a gold spearhead with gold edging within a black oval. This was worn on both lapels of the uniform jacket. There was also a shoulder flash of the same design and colour. Additionally, members of the OSS who operated in England wore the black oval badge.

Bibliography

Adleman, R. H. & George Walton. *Devil's Brigade*. Philadelphia: Chilton, 1966

Admiralty, Grt. Brit. *Royal Marines: Achievement 1940-43*. Aldershot: Gale, 1946

Altieri, James. *Spearheaders* [Darby's Rangers]. New York: Bobbs Merrill, 1960

Anonymous. *History of the 5th Royal Gurkha Rifles* [2 v: 1858-1928,1929-47]. Gale & Polden, 1956

Aurthur, Robert and K. Cohlmia. *Third Marine Division in World War II*. Washington DC: Infantry Journal Press, 1948

Barnes, Major R. M. *Regiments and Uniforms of the British Army*. Seeley Service, 1951

Bando. *Wist Airborne at Normandy*.

Baggaley J. *A Chindit Story* Souvenir Press. 1954

Beevor, J. G. *SOE: Recollections and Reflections, 1940-45*. Bodley Head, 1981

Bidwell, S. *Chindit War* Book Club Associates. 1979

Blair Jr, Clay. *Ridgivay's Paratroopers*. Garden City, NY: The Dial Press, 1980

Blythe, William. *13th Airborne Division*. Atlanta: Albert Love, 1946

Boyle, P. and J. Musgrave Wood. *Jungle, Jungle, Little Chindit*. London: Hollis and Carter, 1944

Breuer, William B. *Geronimo! – U.S. Paratroopers in WWII*. New York: St. Martins, 1989

Brown, Anthony Cave. *Secret War Report of the OSS*. New York: Berkley, 1976

Brown, Arthur. The Jedburghs: A short history (unpublished 1991)

Bruce-Lockhart R. *The Marines Were There* Putnam. 1950

Bryden, John. *Best-Kept Secret: Canadian Secret Intelligence in the Second WW*. Lester

Buckmaster, M. J. *Specially Employed*. Batchword Press, 1952

Buckmaster, Maurice. *They Fought Alone*. Odhams, 1958

Calvert, Michael. *Fighting Mad: One Man's Guerilla War*. Jarrolds, 1964

Campbell B.L. & Reynolds R. *Marine Badges & Insignia of the World* Blanford Press 1983

Capell, Richard. *Simiomata: A Greek Notebook, 1944-5*. London: Macdonald & Co, 1946

Carter, Ross S. *Those Devils in Baggy Pants* [82nd Airborne]. New York: Appleton-Century-Crofts, 1951

Casper, Bernard. *With the Jewish Brigade*. London: Goldston, 1947

Centre of Military History *Merrill's Marauders*. United States Army 1990

Chatterton G. *Wings of Pegasus* Battery Press, Nashville, 1982

Cookridge, E. H. *Set Europe Ablaze: The Inside Story of SOE*. New York: Crowell, 1967

Cole, Howard. *Heraldry In War Formation Badges 1939-1945*. Gale & Polden, 1947

Conner, Howard M. *Spearhead: The World War II History of the 5th Marine Division*. Washington, DC: Infantry Journal Press, 1950

Critchell, Laurence. *Four Stars of Hell* [501st Parachute Infantry Regiment]. New York: McMullen, 1947

Cruickshank, Charles. *SOE in the Far East*. Oxford: Oxford, 1983

Dawson, W. (ed). *Saga of the All American*. Atlanta: Albert Love, 1946

Darby, William O. with W. H. Baumer. *Darby's Rangers: We Led the Way*. Novato: Presidio, 1980

Davis B.L. *British Army Uniforms & Insignia of WW2* Arms & Armour Press. 1993

Dear, Ian *Ten Commando, 1942-45*. New York: St. Martin's, 1987

Devlin G.M. *Paratrooper*. St. Martins Press, New York. 1979

Devlin G.M. *Silent Wings*. St. Martins Press, New York. 1985

Eastwood S., Gray C. & Green A. *When Dragons Flew.* Silver Link Publishing. 1994

Farran, Roy. *Winged Dagger: Adventures on Special Service.* London: Collins, 1948

Fergusson, Bernard. *Beyond the Chindwin.* London: Collins, 1945

Fergusson, Bernard. *Watery Maze: Story of Combined Operations in World War II.* New York: Collins, 1961

Foot M.R.D. *SOE.* BBC Publications 1984 Foot, M. R. D. *SOE: Outline History of the Special Operations Executive,1940-46.* New York: University Publications, 1986

Gale, R. N. *With the 6th Airborne Division in Normandy.* Sampson Low, Marston, 1948

Gaylor, John. *Sons of John Company:* The Indian and Pakistani Armies, 1903-1991. Tunbridge Wells: Spellmount, Ltd, 1992

Graham, A. *Sharpshooters at War.* Sharpshooters Regimental Assn, 1964

Graves, Charles *History of the Royal Ulster Rifles,* volume III: 1919-1948, 1950

Hering PG. *Customs & Traditions of the Royal Air Force.* 1960. Kay R.L.

Hill, John G. *V Corps Operation in the ETO: 6 January 1942-9 May 1945.* Paris: 1945

Historical Committee of the *Brief History of the Special Forces.* Special Forces Club. 1993 Hills R.J.T. *Phantom Was There.* Edward Arnold. 1951

Hogan David W. (jnr) *U.S. Army Special Operations in World War II* US Government Printing Office 1992

Hughes Les *Insignia Of the OSS.* Trading Post Spring 1993

Johnston, Richard W. *Follow Me!* The Story of the Second Marine Division in WWII. New York: Random House, 1948

Karim, MajGen Afsir. *Story of the Indian Airborne Troops.* Spantech Kent R. *First in Parachute Pathfinder Company* Batsford. 1979

King, Michael. *Rangers: Selected Combat Operations in WW II.* Ft. Leavenworth:US Army, 1985

Koskimaki G.E. *The Screaming Eagles* Vantage Press. 1970

Ladd, James *Commandos and Rangers of World War II.* New York: St Martin's Press, 1978

Ladd James D. *SBS The Invisible Raiders* Arms and Armour Press.1983

Landsborough, Gordon. *Tobruk Commando: The Raid to Destroy Rommel's Base.* London: Cassell, 1956

Lepotier, Adolphe *Raiders from the Sea.* London: Kimber, 1954

Long Range Desert Group in Libya War History Branch Department of Internal Affairs New Zealand 1949

Long Range Desert Group in the Mediterranean War History Branch Department of Internal Affairs New Zealand 1950 Longson J. & Taylor C. *Arnhem Odyssey* Pen & Sword Books. 1991

Maund, L.E.H. *Assault from the Sea.* London: Methuen, 1949

McDougall, Murdoch. *Swiftly They Struck: The Story of No. 4 Commando.* London: Arms and Armour, 1954

McGlynn M.B. *Special Service in Greece* War History Branch Department of Internal Affairs New Zealand 1953

Messenger, Charles. *The Commandos 1940-1946* William Kimber. 1985

Messenger, Charles. *The Middle East Commandos* William Kimber. 1988

Neild, Eric. *With Pegasus in India: Story of the 153rd Gurkha Parachute Bn.* Nashville: Battery Press, 1990

Newnham M. *Prelude to Glory* Samson, Low & Marston & Co. 1947

Ogburn Charlton. *The Marauders* Hodder and Stoughton. 1960

Ogburn jr, Charles. *Marauders.* New York: 1959

Otway T.B.H. *Airborne Forces* Imperial War Museum. 1990

Pawley, Margaret. *In Obedience to Instructions.* Leo Cooper, Pen & Sword Books, 1999

Peniakoff, Vladimir. *Popski's Private Army.* London: Cape, 1950

Phillips, C. E. Lucas. *Cockleshell Heroes.* London: 1956

Porter, I. *Operation Autonomous: With the SOE in Wartime Romania*

Purves, T. *The History of the 9th (Parachute)Squadron RE.* 1988
Rentz, Bill *Geronimo:* U.S. Airborne Uniforms, Insignia & Equipment in WWII. Atglen, PA: Schiffer Military History, 1999
Rapport, Leonard and Northwood A. *Rendezvous with Destiny.* Washington, DC Infantry Journal Press, 1948
Rosignoli, G. *Allied Forces in Italy 1943-45* David & Charles Military Books 1989
Routhier, Ray. *The Black Devils, A Pictorial History of the First Special Service Force* 1982
Samain, Bryan. *Commando Men: The Story of a Royal Marine Commando in the North-West.* London: Stevens, 1948
Seth, R. *Lion with Blue Wings* Victor Gollanz. 1955
Sexton, J. *The Marine Raiders* Historical Handbook The American Historical Foundation
Shaw, W. B. Kennedy. *Long Range Desert Group.* London: Greenhill, 1945
Spencer-Chapman F. *The Jungle is Neutral* Chatto and Windus. 1949
Stainforth P. *Wings of the Wind* Falcon Press. 1952
Stevens, G. R. *History of the 2nd King Edward VII's Own Goorkha Rifles,* vol 3. Aldershot: 1952
Strawson J. *The History of the SAS Regiment* Seeker & Warburg. 1984
Taylor, Jeremy *This Band of Brothers: A History of the Reconnaissance Corps.* Bristol: 1947
Thomas M. & Lord C. *New Zealand Army Distinguishing Patches 1911-1991* Part One. Bulletin of The Military Historical Society
US Army. *Merrill's Marauders* (February-May 1944). Washington, DC: GPO, 1945
US Army. *United States Army Special Operations in World War II.* Washington DC: GPO, 1995
Vale, W. L. *History of the South Staffordshire Regiment.* London: Gale & Polden, 1969
Whittaker, Len *Some Talk of Private Armies.* Albanium Publishing Ltd. 1984
Wilcox, W.A. *Chindit Column 76* Longman, Green & Co. Ltd. 1945
Wiles, J. A. *Out of the Clouds* 1984
Wesolowski, Z. P. *Polish Orders Medals Badges and Insignia 1705-1985*

Unpublished Sources (Original copies held in the Taylor Archives)
Report on First Air landing Brigade Operations in Sicily July 1943
Report on Operation Market Garden 1944
Report on Operation Doomsday 1945
Report on Operation Varsi